Michele, 3 R's

Reflect and Recovery and Resolve.

Jeremiah 29:11

Love You, Michael

active. Sharper than any double-edged sword, it pene
n my path. Every *Word of God* is flawless; He is a sl
d of God and obey it. Everyone who hears these *Wo*
the rock. For the *Word of the Lord* is right and tru

God's Word

—— for ——

EVERY NEED

DEVOTIONS FROM THE FATHER'S HEART

he mouth of God. Heaven and earth will pass away, b
gives understanding to the simple. Whoever believes i
the *Word of the Lord* is right and true; He is faithfu
refuge in Him. In God, whose *Word* I praise–in God
ith God, and the *Word* was God. The grass withers a

DESTINY IMAGE® PUBLISHERS, INC.

P.O. Box 310, Shippensburg, PA 17257-0310

"Promoting Inspired Lives"

This book and all other Destiny Image and Destiny Image Fiction books are available at Christian bookstores and distributors worldwide.

Cover design by Eileen Rockwell

Interior design by Terry Clifton

For more information on foreign distributors, call 717-532-3040.

Or reach us on the Internet: www.destinyimage.com

ISBN 13: TP 978-0-7684-1376-2

For Worldwide Distribution, Printed in China

1 2 3 4 5 6 7 8 9 10 11 /19 18 17 16

God's Word for
Every Need

If ever there was a time when we needed ancient, timeless wisdom to help us navigate the challenges of life, it is today. With the institutions and systems of the world being so obviously shaken, people are looking more and more for fixed points in a changing and sometimes unsettling universe.

This is why the God's Word for Every Need series is so timely. The Bible contains wisdom and truth that has stood the test of time. It continues to be the world's best-selling book and the volume that most people reach for when the storms of life strike.

The words of the Bible startle us with their relevance because its ultimate author stands above and beyond time and yet reaches out to His children within time and speaks with a heart of love to them, guiding them through troubled waters, comforting them in the shipwrecks of life.

There is quite simply no other book on the planet that speaks into our day-to-day lives like the Bible.

As you open the pages of this book devoted to *The Father's Heart,* don't think of the words you're about to read as a catalogue of rules and regulations from a harsh and distant God. Think of them as phrases and sentences from the longest love letter in history. Think of them as soothing whispers from a living, loving God.

The Bible is not a legal tome. It is a love letter from Heaven to earth, from our Heavenly Father to His beloved children.

So don't be deceived. *The Father's Heart* may be a small book but it will have a great impact if you let it.

God is about to speak to your needs.

Open your ears and your heart.

Let the Father's tender voice transform your life.

A Heavenly Invitation

"I'll be a Father to you."
—2 CORINTHIANS 6:18

What is the most important verse in the Bible? Many people would answer, "John 3:16: God so loved the world that He gave His one and only Son." However, this verse from Paul's second letter to the church in Corinth can make a very big claim as well. In a way, the entire plan and purpose of God can be summed up in the words, "I'll be a Father to you." This has been God's plan ever since Adam and Eve sinned in the Garden of Eden. When that happened, human beings became separated from the Father's love. In effect, we became spiritual orphans—no longer able to relate to God as our Father. But thanks to Jesus, all that has changed! Jesus is the answer to our orphan state. He came into this world to die for our sins and adopt us into the Father's family on earth. Now we can call God "Father" and rest in His arms of love. In this book of devotions, Jesus is inviting us to respond to these timeless words: "I'll be a Father to you."

PRAYER

Thank You, God, for Your invitation to know You as Father. With all of my heart I say "yes," as I begin this series of devotions. In Jesus' name. Amen.

Our True Identity

"You'll be sons and daughters to me."
—2 CORINTHIANS 6:18

Every good father has a dream for his children. In the previous devotion we saw part of God's dream for us: "I'll be a Father to you." That's been His plan since before the foundation of the world. But there's more. Not only does God want us to know His true identity; He also wants us to know our true identity. If He is our Father, then what does that make us? If we choose to follow His Son, Jesus Christ, it makes us His sons and daughters. This is the greatest joy of all—to know that God is the Father we've all been waiting for, and to revel in the privilege of being His adopted sons and daughters. This is His dream for our lives. Let's make it our highest goal to enter into the fullness of what it means to be the sons and daughters of the greatest Father of all. Let's make it our life's goal to be the best sons and the best daughters that we could possibly be to our Father in Heaven. This is the Father's dream for our lives. Let's make it our dream too!

PRAYER

Dear Father, I thank You that You've called me to be Your adopted child. Help me to build my identity on this wonderful honor. In Jesus' name. Amen.

The Love of All Loves

What marvelous love the Father has extended to us!
—1 JOHN 3:1

There is no greater joy in life than to know that God is our loving Father, yet many people, including those within the Church, have not experienced this unspeakable joy. Many have been wounded by their earthly fathers and, as a result, project their own experience of fatherhood onto God the Father. They then create God in their earthly father's image—seeing God as an absent or abandoning parent. Others have a picture of God as a distant and vengeful Father. None of this is an accurate representation of the picture that Jesus paints. Jesus came to reveal the marvelous love of the Father. Yes, God is King. Yes, God is Lord. Yes, God is Judge. But pre-eminently He is the Father who loved this orphaned planet so deeply that He sent His one and only Son to turn slaves into sons and orphans into heirs. This is the highest blessing of all—to know that God is the world's greatest Father. If you have lacked a good father on earth, know this: you have a perfect Father in Heaven and He has extended His marvelous love to you in Jesus.

PRAYER

Father, I thank You that You are not remote but relational. Help me to enjoy a greater intimacy with You as I read these devotions. In Jesus' name. Amen.

Children of God

Just look at it—we're called children of God!
—1 JOHN 3:1

In the previous devotion we saw that God is the Father who has extended His marvelous love toward us. Directly after emphasizing this, the Apostle John reminds us that we, if we have chosen to follow Jesus, are called "children of God." This is who we really are. This is our true identity. Our self-image is not based on what we do. Our self-worth is not founded on our achievements. No, our true identity is built upon something more lasting and secure. What better foundation than the central revelation of the New Testament—that those who know Jesus are the adopted sons and daughters of the Father? Is that how you see yourself? If not, let me urge you to build your identity on this truth. Let me encourage you to do what the Apostle John says here and "just look at it." Consider, reflect, ponder this truth and then revel in its beauty. If you do, you will always have a profound assurance that your security is in your position as a child of God, not in your work.

PRAYER

Dearest Father, I want to give You praise that You love me for who I am—a child of God. Thank You for this honor. In Jesus' name. Amen.

Demonstrated Affection

"The Father loves you."
—JOHN 16:27

The night before He died, Jesus told His disciples that the Father loved them. The word "love" here does not denote a dutiful concern or a self-forgetful, sacrificial devotion. It carries the sense of "demonstrated affection"—love that's full of warmth and openly shown. This is so important to grasp. The Father's love is not a dutiful or a formal love. No, the sense of Jesus' words here is that "The Father loves you deeply, dearly and demonstrably." What a great love this is! So many earthly fathers are distant, either physically or emotionally. This is not so with our Heavenly Father; when Jesus died and rose again, He ascended to Heaven and from there poured out the Holy Spirit upon His followers. He filled His disciples so full of the Spirit of adoption that they began to cry out "Father!" From that moment on, they knew the Father loved them with a demonstrated affection—with His strong and comforting arms of love. This is what Jesus wants for us too. Let's ask Him to help us to know this in our hearts, not just in our heads. Let's experience the Father's demonstrated affection.

PRAYER

Dear Lord Jesus, I ask You to help me to know in my heart that the Father Himself loves me deeply, dearly and demonstrably. In Your name. Amen.

Just Ask!

"Don't you think the Father who conceived you in
love will give the Holy Spirit when you ask him?"
—LUKE 11:13

How is a person to experience the lavish love and the demonstrated affection of their Father in Heaven? The answer is given in this teaching of Jesus. Jesus has just been talking about earthly fathers. He makes the point that earthly fathers don't give a snake to a son who asks for some fish. If earthly fathers who are imperfect know how to be decent to their children, how much more does our Father in Heaven, who is perfect. All this is very reassuring to us if we are longing to receive the revelation of the Father's heart. In the previous devotion, we saw how Jesus wanted His followers to know that the Father loved them deeply, dearly and demonstrably. For that to happen, we need the same Holy Spirit that the disciples received. We therefore need to ask. When we do, we must remember that God is the best Father in the universe and that He is generous to His children. As you ask, believe that you are already receiving the Father's love through the gift of the Holy Spirit.

PRAYER

*Jesus, You promised that my Father will give me the
Holy Spirit. I ask for that now. Let me encounter the
Father's love. In Your name. Amen.*

The Revealer

"No one knows the Son the way the Father does."
—MATTHEW 11:27

One of the things we have to come to realize, sooner or later, is the fact that Jesus is completely unique in the religions of this world. Jesus stands alone and stands above all other religious leaders and teachers. There are many reasons for this, but the most important of all is the fact that Jesus is the one and only Son of the Father; He is the one and only Son of God *by nature*. No one else can lay claim to be the Father's only Son from eternity to eternity. Yes, you and I may become sons and daughters of God *by adoption*, but Jesus alone is the Father's Son *by nature*. No one else in Heaven or on earth has ever known the Father as He does. In the pantheon of others gods in other religions throughout history, Jesus rises way above them all for being the everlasting Son of the World's Greatest Father. Consequently, other religions may indicate that God is Creator, but Jesus alone reveals that He is the most loving, forgiving, merciful Father of all. If you want to know God as Father, then you have to believe in Jesus as God's Son. He is the only one who can show you.

PRAYER

Dear Lord Jesus, I confess that You are the only Son of God and that You died so that I might come to the Father. I believe in You. In Your name. Amen.

Everyone's Included

> "I'm not keeping it to myself; I'm ready to go over
> it line by line with anyone willing to listen."
> —MATTHEW 11:27

What is Jesus referring to here? If you read the previous devotion you will know that He is talking about knowing God as Father. Jesus has just declared that the only one who knows the Father is the Son, but He goes on to say that He's not keeping this to Himself. He is ready to lead anyone who is teachable into a personal and intimate friendship with the Father. This in itself highlights the enormous gulf between what Jesus offers and what everyone else offers. Others offer religion, but Jesus offers relationship. Others offer rules and rituals, but Jesus offers something more than the outward form of religion. He offers the inner, powerful reality of an intimate communion with our Father in Heaven. What a gift that is! We no longer carry the heavy burden of trying to please God through our self-effort, through our works. We can simply come to Jesus and receive the light-fitting mantle of His freely given love—a love that is available to everyone who is willing to listen.

PRAYER

Jesus, I am willing to listen. Please mentor me in what it means to know the Father's love. Teach me line by line. In Your precious name. Amen.

A Humble Heart

> "Thank you, Father, Lord of heaven and earth. You've concealed your ways from sophisticates and know-it-alls, but spelled them out clearly to ordinary people."
> —MATTHEW 11:25

One of the saddest things is seeing someone who has a lot of theology but little to no intimacy. They lecture people about God and His ways but their knowledge is theoretical. It is not heartfelt. It is propositional knowledge (knowledge about God) rather than personal knowledge (knowledge based on relationship with Abba Father). This was also true in Jesus' day. The theologians of His time knew something about God as Father. There are, after all, hints concerning God's Fatherhood in the Old Testament. There was enough revelation about the Father heart of God in the Hebrew Scriptures to help them know the Father in a personal not just an intellectual way. Yet they had no real relationship with the Father. However, the disciples—who were untrained when it came to theology—came to know the Father's love in a very real way. This shows that you don't have to have great intellect to know the Father. You just have to have a humble heart. If we are proud, there is every chance that we will end up sound in doctrine but sound asleep.

PRAYER

Lord Jesus, don't let my intellect get in the way of knowing the Father. I humble myself and ask You to help me. In Your name. Amen.

The Old Revealed

God, you are our Father.
—ISAIAH 64:8

We saw in the previous devotion that there are hints about the Father heart of God in the Old Testament. The Jewish leaders and scholars of Jesus' day had enough hints about the Fatherhood of God in their Scriptures to have learned to know Him more than cognitively—in their heads. In the coming devotions we are going to look at many of these Old Testament revelations of the Father heart of God. Here is a perfect example. The prophet Isaiah declares that God is our Father. This shows that the ancient maxim is true: the Old Testament is the New concealed while the New Testament is the Old revealed. In other words, what is implied in the Old Testament is explicitly stated in the New. Nowhere is this truer than in the case of the Father heart of God. Isaiah caught a glimpse of the wonderful truth that God can be called "Father," but it was Jesus Christ, over 500 years later, who taught us to know and to say "Our Father in Heaven." Isaiah saw partially; Jesus saw completely. Jesus gives us the total picture of what we can know about the Father.

PRAYER

Thank You, Jesus, for showing us a complete picture of the Father's love. Please help me to declare, "God, You are my Father." In Your name. Amen.

Our Living Father

You're our living Father, our Redeemer,
famous from eternity!
—Isaiah 63:16

There are so many names for God. Some of these are prefaced by the word *Jehovah,* a name that means something like "Forever," or "Always." Others are prefaced by the word *El* which means "God." Here are some common titles for God in the Old Testament: *Jehovah Rapha* means, "The God who Heals." *Jehovah Shammah* means "The God who is There." *Jehovah Shalom* means, "The God who is Peace." Then there are other titles like *El Olam,* "The Everlasting God," and *El Shaddai,* "The Lord God Almighty." Then there are other titles such as *Adonai* meaning "Lord" and *Elohim,* "God." There are descriptive terms like "Rock," "Fortress," and "Redeemer." Towering above them all, however, is the name that we find 15 times in the Old Testament and 165 times on the lips of Jesus: "Father." This is the most important name for God, not only in the Bible but also in the entire sweep of human history. As Isaiah proclaims, God is "our living Father." He is the Father who lives for all eternity. There is no higher title you can give to Him than that.

PRAYER

Dear God, thank You not only that You are my Father but that You're alive. Teach me to talk with You as a child to their loving Dad. In Jesus' name. Amen.

Being a Blessing

"I'll make you a great nation and bless you. I'll make
you famous; you'll be a blessing. I'll bless those who
bless you; those who curse you I'll curse. All the
families of the Earth will be blessed through you."
—GENESIS 12:2–3

We see the Father's heart so clearly in the life of Abraham. At this
stage, he is called "Abram," which means "high father." He is 75
years old when God calls him. God says that He's going to form
a nation out of Abram's descendants and that He's going to bless
His people. He goes on to say that through this one nation—
later called Israel—He will bless all the nations of the earth. Here
the Father tells Abram that this nation is destined to walk in the
Father's love and to give that love away to every people group
under the sun. This is the Father's heart for all those who follow
Jesus. We are not just to be blessed by the Father's love. We are to
be a blessing too.

PRAYER

*Dear Father, help me to be so filled with Your love that
I cannot resist giving it away to others, especially to
those who don't know You. In Jesus' name. Amen.*

Saying Yes

"Look at the sky. Count the stars. Can
you do it? Count your descendants! You're
going to have a big family, Abram!"
—GENESIS 15:5

It was hard for Abram to believe that God would give him a son,
and that through this son's descendants, God would create a
great nation. Abram was 75 years old. How could he impregnate
his wife Sarah? Knowing that Abram was struggling, the Father
told him to look at the stars in the night sky and to count them.
There were too many to number. God then told him, "That's
how many descendants you're going to have from the son born
from your body." The Bible tells us that Abram believed God and
that this faith meant that he enjoyed from this moment a right
relationship with his Heavenly Father. Here we see the Father's
heart. The Father wanted to create a great nation out of Abram's
offspring. That was His plan. But in order for this plan to come
to pass, Abram had to give his "yes" to God's calling. Let's resolve
to say "yes" to the Father's heart for us—always!

PRAYER

*Dear Father, I thank You that You have a plan for my
life, and that I'm never too old to activate it. Help me
always to say "yes" to Your plans for my life. Amen.*

Learning to Wait

> When Abram was ninety-nine years old, God
> showed up and said to him, "I am The Strong God,
> live entirely before me, live to the hilt! I'll make a
> covenant between us and I'll give you a huge family."
> —GENESIS 17:1–2

What age does the opening verse tell us Abram was at this point? The answer is 99 years old. How old was Abram when God gave him the original calling to become a father to many nations? The answer is 75. This means that Abram had been waiting just under a quarter of a century for the promise to be fulfilled. That's a long time! Often when we receive a sense of the Father's calling on our lives we fail to recognize that there may well be a substantial amount of time between the giving of the word and its activation. Our Father wants us to learn how to go on trusting even when the evidence is seemingly stacked against the promise being fulfilled. This is what faith is—it is continuing to believe in something even when we cannot yet see it.

PRAYER

Dear Father, teach me how to go on believing in Your promises over my life, even when I cannot see any signs of their fulfillment. In Jesus' name. Amen.

Identity and Destiny

> "You'll be the father of many nations. Your name
> will no longer be Abram, but Abraham, meaning
> that 'I'm making you the father of many nations.'"
> —GENESIS 17:4–5

Up until now, God has used *Abram,* a name which in Hebrew means, "high father." Now He changes to *Abraham,* which means "father of multitudes." Here we see the Father teaching Abraham lessons about identity and destiny. Abraham's identity is to be a father who identifies with the Father heart of God. His destiny is to have a son and through this son to have as many descendants as there are stars in the night sky. A similar process happens to Sarah. Originally, she is called *Sarai,* meaning "My princess," but God renames her *Sarah,* "mother of nations." Here again we see the Father's heart. First, He reveals identity ("you're a princess") then destiny ("you're a mother of nations"). Only by drawing close to the Father's heart do we get to know who we truly are and what our purpose really looks like.

PRAYER

*Dear Father, teach me to understand my true identity
and through that to come to learn what Your destiny is
for my life. In Jesus' name. Amen.*

The Promise~Keeper

"I'm establishing my covenant between me and you, a covenant that includes your descendants, a covenant that goes on and on and on, a covenant that commits me to be your God and the God of your descendants."
—GENESIS 17:7

Many children experience the disappointment of having a father who makes promises but fails to keep them. When it comes to our Heavenly Father, we need to remember that He is a Father who always delivers on His promises. This is why He is keen to stress to Abraham that He is making a *covenant* with him and that He is bound to keep this covenant come what may. What a great reassurance this was to Abraham. What a great reassurance it is to us. If you had an earthly dad who didn't keep his word when he told you he was going to do something for you, know that your Father in Heaven is not like this at all. He is a covenant-making, promise-keeping Father. When He promises to bless you, He means to keep His word. It's just a matter of time.

PRAYER

Dear God, I am so deeply grateful that You are the perfect Father and that when You promise to bless me, You will surely keep Your word. In Jesus' name. Amen.

The Gift of Laughter

"Your wife, Sarah, will have a baby, a
son. Name him Isaac (Laughter)."
—GENESIS 17:19

There is something we need to understand about the Father heart of God: He has plans to prosper us in such a way that we can live life in all its fullness whatever our circumstances. His intention is to bring us joy and to make us joy-bringers to others, even in tough times. This is what Abraham's story reveals. Yes, Abraham and Sarah had to wait until they were 100 years old before the promise over their lives was fulfilled. But when it was, their inheritance was one of joy. That is why the Father tells Abraham and Sarah to name their child Isaac—which means "Laughter." What a beautiful picture that is of the Father's heart. When we go on believing His promises even when we can see no evidence of them being fulfilled, one day we get the reward of seeing the thing for which we have gone on believing. When that happens, laughter is birthed in our soul. Let us never forget: God is a Father who wants us to be full of joy. Let's laugh a little today. That's what faithful sons and daughters do.

PRAYER

*Dear Father, thank You that the reward of believing
is to experience the joy and laughter of seeing Your
promises fulfilled. In Jesus' name. Amen.*

Strangers From Heaven

God appeared to Abraham at the Oaks of Mamre
while he was sitting at the entrance of his tent.
It was the hottest part of the day. He looked up
and saw three men standing. He ran from his
tent to greet them and bowed before them.
—GENESIS 18:1–2

As he is living at the Oaks of Mamre, Abraham is visited by three men who turn out to be more than they seem. Who are they? The answer is that they are a manifestation on earth of the three persons of God. In the New Testament, we learn that God is three persons who share one substance or being. God is therefore triune. He is the Father, the Son and the Holy Spirit. As Abraham prepares to receive the fulfillment of his prophetic word, he sees the three persons of God appearing to him in the heat of the noonday sun. When he does, he rushes to greet and bow down to them. No wonder God chose Abraham. Here was someone who instinctively knew how to welcome and worship the Three-in-One God.

PRAYER

*Help me, O God, to welcome and to worship You as the
Father, Son and Holy Spirit. Would You help me to
encounter You today. In Jesus' name. Amen.*

A Painful Privilege

He said, "Take your dear son Isaac whom you
love and go to the land of Moriah. Sacrifice
him there as a burnt offering on one of the
mountains that I'll point out to you."
—GENESIS 22:2

Abraham's son Isaac has been born to him and Sarah. Now
it looks as if it really will come to pass that Abraham will have
countless descendants. Then, out of the blue, God tells Abraham
to go to Mount Moriah and sacrifice his son as a burnt offering.
Abraham must have been in terrible distress. Why would the
Father ask Abraham to do such a thing? The clue is in the phrase
"your dear son." This is a translation of a Hebrew word meaning
"one and only," "precious," "special." It is the word that John will
translate into Greek when he writes the prologue to his Gospel
and describes Jesus as the "one-of-a-kind" Son of God. This is the
clue. Abraham is being granted a glimpse of what it will be like
for our Father in Heaven when He gives up His own "Dear Son"
on the mount of crucifixion. Abraham will feel perplexed now.
One day, in Heaven, he will feel very privileged.

PRAYER

*Thank You, Dear Father, for showing us through
Abraham the pain You endured when Your Son was
crucified. Thank You for Your astounding love. Amen.*

Passing the Test

> "I swear—God's sure word!—because you
> have gone through with this, and have not
> refused to give me your son, your dear, dear
> son, I'll bless you—oh, how I'll bless you!"
> —GENESIS 22:16–17

Just as Abraham is about to sacrifice his son Isaac, an angel appears and orders Abraham to stay his hand. Abraham has proved to the Father that there is no sacrifice he will not make if God asks him. What has most impressed God here is Abraham's holy and healthy fear of the Lord. What does the Bible mean by "the fear of the Lord"? It means being so in awe at our Father's sovereign authority that when He asks us to do something, we will do it, however much it costs. Here we see how important it is not only to love God as our Father but also to obey God as our King. We must not only draw near to Him in intimacy but also bow low before Him with humility. As John Wesley once said, there are many who fear the Lord, some who love the Lord, but precious few who both love and fear Him. Abraham did just that. He both loved and feared God. When our faithful Father asks us to surrender all for Him, will we love Him enough to say "yes" too?

PRAYER

*Thank You, God, that You are not just my affectionate
Father. You are also my awesome King. Teach me to be
Your subject as well as Your son. Amen.*

Behold the Ram

Abraham looked up. He saw a ram caught by its
horns in the thicket. Abraham took the ram and
sacrificed it as a burnt offering instead of his son.
—GENESIS 22:13

As Abraham passes his test of faith and obedience, the Father
provides a substitute. In the thicket nearby, a ram has become
entangled in the branches. Abraham senses what needs to be
done. God has asked for a sacrifice but has made it clear that Isaac
is not the one. Now a surrogate is provided. The ram supplies the
need. Many hundreds of years later, there will be a not dissimi-
lar scenario played out on the Mount of Crucifixion. Jesus Christ
will take our place. He will die the death that we deserved. He
will be the Lamb of God who takes away the sin of the world.
Instead of us being the offering, Jesus will offer Himself to the
Father as a propitiation for our sins. In His body, He will absorb
the Father's righteous anger at our sin. He who will know no sin
in His entire life will become sin for our sakes. Do you see how
Abraham is led into the deepest places of the Father's heart?

PRAYER

*Thank You, Jesus, for being the Lamb of God the
Father has provided so that we might not die in our sin
but live in Your righteousness. Amen.*

Treasured by God

God, your God, chose you out of all the people on
Earth for himself as a cherished, personal treasure.
—DEUTERONOMY 7:6

It's so important to realize why the Father chose the people of
Israel. This was not because Israel had better credentials than
the other nations. In fact, there was nothing on Israel's side that
merited this kind of attention and affection. Rather, it was the
Father's choice—a choice motivated simply by love. The Father
wanted to embrace Israel as His children, purely because He
longed for a people for Himself—a people that He cherished and
treasured in a special way. This is what makes the history of Israel
so poignant. Instead of walking in the Father's love and giving it
away—which had been the Father's plan since the beginning—
Israel rejected this perfect Father. This is a caution to all of us
who follow Jesus. We need to remember that there is nothing
more rewarding than to be the Father's cherished, personal treasure. He alone satisfies.

PRAYER

*Dearest Father, thank You that You call me "cherished"
and "Your treasure." Nothing else compares to that and
I worship You. Amen.*

Small Is Beautiful

God wasn't attracted to you and didn't choose you because you were big and important—the fact is, there was almost nothing to you. He did it out of sheer love.
—Deuteronomy 7:7–8

Here is something comforting about the Father's heart. He didn't choose Israel because Israel was important. He chose Israel out of "sheer love." What a reminder this is about the Father's love! If it had been us, we might have chosen the Egyptians because of their pyramids, the Greeks because of their wisdom, or the Romans because of their armies. But the Israelites had nothing like this to commend them. They were nomads in the desert when the Father called them through Abraham to be His people. This should be an abiding lesson for all of us. There is nothing we can do to make the Father love us any more than He does already. He has already chosen to place His affections upon us. All we have to do is receive His love. We do not need to strive to earn it. We simply need to rest in it and rejoice!

PRAYER

Dear loving, Heavenly Father, thank You so much for the "sheer love" You have shown me. I choose to rest in this love. In Jesus' name. Amen.

The Adopting Father

"Then you are to tell Pharaoh, 'God's
Message: Israel is my son, my firstborn!'"
—Exodus 4:22

In Bible times, a Roman couple who couldn't have children often adopted a son from a family of slaves. For the boy born into slavery, this was a great break! Not only would he be rescued from poverty. He would also be granted a new father, a new family and a new freedom. He would also inherit everything! This is precisely why the Apostle Paul talked about adoption as Israel's greatest privilege (see Rom. 9:4). When God chose Israel, He adopted one nation from all the earth. He lavished love on a people who didn't deserve it. This is why God told Moses to go and tell Pharaoh, "Israel is my firstborn son." God had granted Israel the status and privilege of the eldest son in the family. What an indescribable honor this is! This is truly the Father's heart!

PRAYER

Thank You, Dearest Father, for adopting me into Your family and giving me the privilege and honor of being Your child. In Jesus' name. Amen.

Drawing Near

"The whole Earth is mine to choose from, but
you're special: a kingdom of priests, a holy nation."
—EXODUS 19:5–6

Here we see the Father's heart on full display! God tells Moses to go and tell His people that He has chosen Israel to be "a kingdom of priests." The word translated "priest" here is the Hebrew word *cohen* which literally means "one who draws near." The Father's heart all along was for the children of Israel to know Him in a deeply relational way and to draw near to Him in love. The Bible teaches us that if we draw near to this loving Father, He will draw near to us (see James 4:8, NASB). Let's resolve to be a Kingdom of *cohanim*—a royal family of adopted sons and daughters of God who love to draw near to the Father. When we approach our Father with affection in our hearts and adoration on our lips, He promises to approach us and to embrace us in His arms. What a good, good Father we have. Let's make a practice of drawing near to Him.

PRAYER

*Father, I want to be in a Kingdom of those who
draw near to You. Help me to cultivate a lifestyle of
approaching You with love in Jesus' name. Amen.*

Glowing With Glory

And God spoke with Moses face-to-face.
—Exodus 33:11

If there was ever anyone in the Old Testament who loved drawing near to the Father, it was Moses. Moses set up a Tent of Meeting outside a camp containing approximately 1.2 million people. He did so because he wanted to meet regularly with the Father away from the crowd. When he did, Moses spoke with God "face-to-face." The word translated "face" also means "presence." Moses was fully present to the Father and the Father was fully present to Moses—so much so, in fact, that Moses' own face would glow afterwards. Sometimes we mistakenly think that intimacy with the Father was only possible after Jesus. But Moses' example shows that even before Jesus came there were heroes of faith who were friends of God—shining ones whose countenances showed the afterglow of contact with the Father. Let's be children who seek the Father's face and who radiate His smile.

PRAYER

Father I long to be like Moses and enjoy a close friendship with You; help me to seek Your face and to glow with Your glory. In Jesus' name. Amen.

The Father's Smile

God bless you and keep you,
God smile on you and gift you,
God look you full in the face
and make you prosper.
—NUMBERS 6:24–26

This is the oldest blessing in history and it is truly the Father's blessing. Moses is instructed by God to tell Aaron to give this blessing over the people. Notice those simple words, "God smile on you." When you think of your loving, Heavenly Father, how do you imagine Him? Do you see him frowning with anger? Or do you see Him smiling with pride and joy? Many people have only known earthly fathers who looked with disappointment or dismay at them—maybe displeasure or disengagement too. God is not like that. Yes, He is displeased with us if we sin, but when we are walking in His ways and His will, He consistently looks at us with a love as vast as the ocean and a smile as wide as the heavens. This is because He is so delighted that we are His children. He is so thrilled that we belong to Him. Let's resolve to dwell under the blessing of the Father's smiling countenance every day.

PRAYER

Thank You, Father, that You look upon me with delight. Help me to revel in the blessing of Your smiling face every day and night. In Jesus' name. Amen.

A Wayward Son

"When Israel was only a child, I loved him.
I called out, 'My son!'—called him out of Egypt.
But when others called him,
he ran off and left me."
—HOSEA 11:1–2

When Israel was a very young nation, God delivered His people out of Egypt. This act of rescue is described through the prophet Hosea as an act in which God called His son out of Egypt. Notice the word "son." God adopted Israel out of all the nations of the earth to enjoy the status of a son. But here's the thing—this son chose to rebel against the Father's love. This son ran off and abandoned his father when other gods enticed him. This is why God had to send Jesus. Jesus, as the Son of God, had to show us what a true son looks like. He had to show once and for all that God is called our Father and we are called to be His faithful children.

PRAYER

Dear God, thank You for giving us all another chance to know You as Father. Help me to be a faithful child and follow You alone. In Jesus' name. Amen.

Our Father's Arms

"You saw what he did in the wilderness, how God,
your God, carried you as a father carries his child."
—DEUTERONOMY 1:31

When God rescued the Israelites from their slavery in Egypt, He carried His people as a father carries his child on his shoulders. What a beautiful description that is! It highlights the fact that right from the beginning God has wanted to be a Father to His children. The tragedy is that God's people in the Old Testament ran after foreign gods. Instead of allowing the Father's love to carry and sustain them, they looked for idols or counterfeit affections. This is a warning to all of us. We can try and find comfort in unhealthy and toxic attachments or we can seek true solace from the healthiest attachment of all—to our Father in Heaven. Israel's history is a reminder: let's choose the Father's love every time. It will carry us through every desert.

PRAYER

*Dear Father, I choose to be carried by Your love and
Your love alone. I reject counterfeit affections and set
my heart on Yours alone. In Jesus' name. Amen.*

Carried by Love

*"You have seen what I did to Egypt and how I carried
you on eagles' wings and brought you to me."*
—EXODUS 19:4

In the previous devotion, we saw how Moses described God as a father who carries his children. Let us look a little more closely at the word "carry." The Old Testament was mainly written in Hebrew. The Hebrew word for "carry," in both Exodus 19:4 and Deuteronomy 1:31, is *nasa*. What is meant by this verb? Picture a father for a moment. His small child is walking by his side. The father stoops down, picks the child up in his arms, and lifts him to his chest. There he holds him very close. In the general course of our lives as the children of God, God walks with us as a father walks with his child, holding our hand. But then there are those special moments—moments of great joy—when He lifts us up and we feel His embrace. This is a *nasa* moment. When Father carries us to the highest heights of His love, He takes us beyond any NASA spacecraft. What an uplifting thing it is to be carried by the Father's love!

PRAYER

*Dear Father, thank You that You always walk with me.
I ask that You would lift me up and hold me close to
Your heart. In Jesus' name. Amen.*

Faithful Children

Isn't this your Father who created you, who
made you and gave you a place on Earth?
—DEUTERONOMY 32:6

You can hear the pain in Moses' voice here. He is talking to the
people of Israel shortly before he dies. He reminds the people
about how God has loved them like a father, finding them in the
desert and adopting them, holding them by the hand and guiding them in the way they should go. This is a beautiful metaphor
of how the Father chose and adopted Israel out of all the nations
of the earth and led them out of slavery in Egypt into the privilege of adopted sonship in the Promised Land. Now, however,
they are making and following after idols. How can people who
have been lavished with such love reject it? How can we believe
that there is anything that could begin to compete with this
Father's love? This is the perversity of the human heart. We know
that the Love of all loves is the only thing that truly satisfies but
we insist on running after counterfeit and toxic affections. Let's
choose the Father's love over love for the things of this world.
Let's be faithful children.

PRAYER

Father, help me always to remember that it is You who
created me, You who gave me a place on this earth, You
alone who truly satisfies the soul. Amen.

A Father's Discipline

God disciplines you in the same ways
a father disciplines his child.
—DEUTERONOMY 8:5

In the Old Testament, the people of Israel were given the supreme honor of being the nation adopted by God. Sadly, they forgot that they were called to obey God rather than do their own thing. They chose to set their affections on foreign gods instead of the Father who had set His affections on them. Seasons of rebelling against the Father's love were therefore followed by seasons of being refined by that love. This is what is meant by "discipline." Our Father's discipline is never excessive, violent, abusive or unjustified. It is always measured, kind, loving and deserved. When Israel was disobedient, God addressed this "as a father disciplines his child." This teaches us something immensely important about the Father's heart. Not only does God have the capacity to dote on us when we are faithful. He also has the capacity to discipline us when we are faithless. Let's try to be sons and daughters who do not need seasons of discipline.

PRAYER

*Dearest Father, help me to live according to Your ways
and to be so faithful to Your will that I do not need
constantly to be disciplined. In Jesus' name. Amen.*

What's in a Name?

There was a man from the tribe of Benjamin named
Kish. He was the son of Abiel, grandson of Zeror.
—1 Samuel 9:1

The revelation of the Father heart of God comes in different ways
in the Old Testament. Sometimes it comes directly, when people
address God as "Father." At other times, it comes more indirectly,
in references to Israel, various kings, as God's son. Occasionally
it comes even more indirectly, in the names fathers gave to their
children. Here's an example. A man called Zeror gave his baby
boy the name *Abiel*. *Abi* in Hebrew means "Father." *El* means
"God." The name *Abiel* accordingly means "My Father is God!"
This kind of thing happens frequently in ancient Israel, which
is why we see names like *Abinadab* (My Father is Generous),
Abiezer (My Father is a Help), and *Abijah* (My Father is Yahweh).
What a wonderful thing it is to know that My Father is God, my
Father is Generous, my Father is my Help, and that my Father
is Yahweh!

PRAYER

*Dear Father, I love the fact that You're not only my
Father; You're also my God, my generous provider, my
ever-present helper, my great "I Am." Amen.*

A Royal Son

"He'll call out, 'Oh, my Father—my God,
my Rock of Salvation!'"
--PSALM 89:26

During Israel's history, there was one whom the Bible describes as a man after God's own heart. That man was David, Israel's greatest king. When God chose David, He chose a man whom He knew would love Him. Even though He also knew that David would make mistakes, He also foresaw that the call would be greater than the fall and that David would never lose his love for God. This is reflected in the words God speaks here about David: "He'll call out, 'Oh, my Father.'" Notice the little word "my." David was someone who enjoyed a personal and intimate relationship with his Heavenly Father. Yes, he was a leader, but before that, he was a lover. Yes he was a warrior, but before that he was a worshipper—a worshipper of the one whom he addressed with feeling as, "Oh, my Father!" David was truly a royal son. Let's be men and women after God's own heart and daily cry out, "Oh, my Father!"

PRAYER

Thank You, Jesus, for the example of King David's devotion to his Heavenly Father. Give me a Davidic heart of worship, I pray. In Your name. Amen.

Away From the Crowd

"Step out of the traffic! Take a long,
loving look at me, your High God."
—PSALM 46:10

King David discovered the importance of stepping away from the noise and crowds and spending time in stillness and quiet with his Father in Heaven. His highest priority and his greatest passion was to set himself apart from the business of his daily life and to simply spend time as a child before his Father, taking a long, loving look at God. This is something we all need to cultivate in our lives. Many of us get drawn into the whirlpool of daily duties, whether at work or at home, whether with colleagues or with children. By the time the day is done, all we have managed is a few prayers asking for help, uttered under our breath on the go. There is nothing wrong with such prayers. They are a very important part of our conversation with our Father. But we must also take care to have a calm oasis each day, where we can rest in the Father's presence, gaze upon His smiling countenance, and enjoy the good news that He loves us for who we *are* more than what we *do*.

PRAYER

*Dearest Father, please help me to carve out some space
and time each day when I can step out of the traffic and
step into Your loving presence. Amen.*

Basking in the Son

One day spent in your house, this beautiful
place of worship, beats thousands
spent on Greek island beaches.
—PSALM 84:10

The psalmist loved the Father's presence more than anything else. He loved spending time away from his daily duties, stilling his beating heart, finding a place of serenity in a very busy life. Where did he do this? The answer is, not in his house, but in the Father's house. He simply accessed the Father's presence in the Father's house. One day spent there, simply adoring the Father and giving Him the highest praise, was better for him than thousands on a Greek island. This is a very telling statement. Today, so many people spend so much money trying to find fun in the sun on their holidays. The psalmist understood that you don't need to break the bank or travel to far off islands to find true rest. True rest involves finding a place of tranquility, a place where you can enjoy the Father's presence. And good news, it's FREE! Let's never forget, it's better to be drenched in the Son than it is in the sun.

PRAYER

*Dearest Father, help me to create a space in my life
where I can rest in Your presence and bask in the light of
Your Son. In His name. Amen.*

After God's Heart

Father of orphans,
champion of widows,
is God in his holy house.
—PSALM 68:5

What is the evidence that King David was a man after the Father heart of God? Here we see at least one of the clues. David understood that people of Israel had been like a child without a father, but God had adopted them because He is supremely a Father to the fatherless. This is why David wrote this psalm or song of worship. He saw something by revelation. He understood, from his own intimate communion, something about the heart of God. He recognized that God is supremely a Dad to those who have lost their dads. That is why, throughout the Old Testament, we find so many verses in which God tells His people to look after orphans. Let's follow David's example and give voice to our love for the Father to the fatherless. And let's turn that worship into action by giving help to orphans and widows.

PRAYER

Dear God, I give You praise that You are a Father to those who do not know an earthly father's love. Help me to reflect Your heart. In Jesus' name. Amen.

Holding Us Close

My father and mother walked out and left me,
but God took me in.
—PSALM 27:10

King David knew that parents sometimes abandon their children. What happens when a child is left by their father and mother? They feel abandoned. How is this wound to be healed? You can have all the counseling and medication in the world, you can try and turn negative thoughts into positive ones, but in the final analysis there is only one truly effective and lasting treatment—to fall into the arms of your Father in Heaven. This is what David saw by revelation. A negative experience of being fathered can only ultimately be displaced by a positive experience of being fathered. That positive experience comes when our Father takes us in or, more precisely, "holds us close." Only an encounter with the enfolding arms of Father God will ultimately fill the hole in our wounded hearts.

PRAYER

*Father, I bring my wounds to You today. Please hold me
in Your arms and heal me, through the amazing grace
of Your loving embrace. In Jesus' name. Amen.*

Always There

He won't let you down; He won't leave you
—DEUTERONOMY 31:6

We live in a fatherless world today. On every continent and in every nation there is a pandemic of fatherlessness. This lack of fathering can take many forms. Sometimes children have fathers who abuse them, through their words and their actions. Others have fathers who are away all the time, or who are emotionally away even while they are physically present. Others have fathers who are more in love with their addictions than they are with them. Still others have fathers who walk out on them. All of these scenarios are played out time and time again throughout the earth. But the truth is this: we have a Father in Heaven who will never let us down and who will never leave us. That is what Moses saw thousands of years ago. That is what he declared to God's people. If we have been wounded by our earthly dads, we need to remember we have a Heavenly Father who is always true to His promises, always there for us.

PRAYER

Thank You, oh my Father, for the reassurance that You are completely trustworthy, and that You promise never to leave me. Amen.

The Book of My Heart

I'm an open book to you;
even from a distance, you know what I'm thinking.
—PSALM 139:2

It's hard not to admire David's heart. He seems to have had the most extraordinarily intimate relationship with the Father—a relationship in which he knew, through heartfelt communion and authentic worship, how the Father saw him. This is one of the key things to remember about the Father's heart. He longs for us not only to see Him as He really is, but to see ourselves as He sees us too. This is why Psalm 139 is one of the best loved passages in the Bible. Here we catch a glimpse of the Father's heart toward David. David saw by revelation of the Holy Spirit that his life was like "an open book" before God. God saw everything. He saw the joys and the sorrows and He saw the secret things as well as the surface things. What an amazing Father we have. Even from Heaven He knows our hearts and He hears our thoughts. Let's allow Him to look into our hearts every day and to show us what needs changing in order for us to be a book that glorifies Him!

PRAYER

Dear Father, I bring my heart to You today, holding it like a book in my hands. Make my heart one with Yours. In Jesus' name. Amen.

An Original Story

Like an open book, you watched me grow
from conception to birth; all the stages of
my life were spread out before you.
—PSALM 139:16

King David celebrates the fact that God is the best author in the universe and that He knows how the story of our lives turns out. The best stories have three acts—a beginning, a middle and an end. When David sang this song, he knew that God had already written all three parts of the story, even though David himself was only about half way through it. He had written the beginning, the middle and the end. Isn't it comforting to know that our loving Heavenly Father is the most creative author of all? He has already planned out the plotline of our lives. He has decided in advance the kind of character He wants to develop in us. He has written in us a bests elling, award-winning, original story! Let's entrust our lives to the Divine Author and allow Him to fashion our story into His story, so that our Father alone gets the glory!

PRAYER

*Thank You, Dear Father, that You already know my
story and that my story is unlike anyone else's. Let the
story unfold according to Your perfect will. Amen.*

Divine Editing

God rewrote the text of my life
when I opened the book of my heart to his eyes.
—PSALM 18:24

Our Father is the greatest author of all and He has already written the story of our lives. At times, however, we fail and fall. King David did when he committed adultery and murder. But when he repented, the Father came and studied the book of David's heart and, like a careful and meticulous editor, began to rewrite it. David's story was subjected to such a remarkable piece of divine editing that when the New Testament came to sum up his life it didn't describe him as an adulterer or a murderer, but as "a man after God's own heart" (see Acts 13:22). Now that's what I call "divine editing." Whenever I repent, my loving Father rewrites the text of my life in such a loving, gracious and forgiving way that it is not my failures that define me, but my deep-down heart of love for Him. What a good, good Father He is!

PRAYER

I love You, Dearest Father, for the way that You so kindly rewrite the text of my life so that my story showcases Your amazing grace. In Jesus' name. Amen.

Generational Intimacy

"He'll be my royal adopted son and I'll be his father."
—1 CHRONICLES 22:10

There are bad things that we can leave as a legacy, as parents—but there are also good things. In King David's case, he didn't provide a healthy example when it came to marriage relationships, which is why subsequent generations suffered from dysfunctional family life. However, there was also something very healthy that he passed on—his passionate love for his Father. God made sure that the goodness of this intimacy would be transmitted to his son Solomon, who became king after David and who fulfilled David's dream of building the Temple in Jerusalem. To this son, God promised David, "I'll be a father to him." What a timely reminder to us all. Our longing and love for the Father's heart will not just be restricted to our own relationship with God. It is something that can be passed on to our children too. They can become royally adopted daughters and sons.

PRAYER

Dear Father, help me to have such a passion for Your heart that it proves contagious to my children and their children. In Jesus' name. Amen.

Steadfast Love

"Take heart! Don't be anxious or get discouraged.
God, my God, is with you in this; he won't
walk off and leave you in the lurch."
—1 CHRONICLES 28:20

What a wonderful thing it is when a father blesses his son. That is precisely what is happening here. King David is passing on to his son Solomon a comforting truth. What is that? It is the simple truth that when our Father gives us a task to do, He will be right at our side helping us, until every last detail has been completed. This is exactly what Solomon needed to hear. Once David had died, he was going to take on the responsibility of building the Temple in Jerusalem—a building that Jesus was later going to call "my Father's house." This was a huge undertaking. I'm sure that when the going got tough he remembered the words of his dad and his anxiety lifted. What a great truth David is here passing on to the next generation. Let's be sure to tell our sons and daughters of the Father's steadfast love.

PRAYER

*Thank You Father, that when You give us a
responsibility, You give us the resources, and with them
Your reassurance. In Jesus' name. Amen.*

Wisdom From Heaven

Pay close attention, friend,
to what your father tells you.
—PROVERBS 1:8

When King David had died, his son Solomon became king. One of the greatest gifts Solomon possessed was that of wisdom. He wrote what is known as the Book of Proverbs in the Bible. These proverbs are short and precise words of wisdom from Heaven. They are life principles that Solomon received by the Holy Spirit as he listened to his Father in Heaven. Solomon, as God's royally adopted son, had access to timeless truths designed to help people reign in life. Solomon heard and obeyed what his Father said. He then passed this wisdom on to others. As I read the Book of Proverbs, I position myself as a royally adopted son before my Heavenly Father and seek to pay close attention to what my Father tells me. When I hear and obey His instructions, I am empowered to bring my Father's rule into both my character and my circumstances. This should be the greatest dream of our lives—to be a faithful and fruitful child of the King of kings.

PRAYER

Dear Father, help me always to pay close attention to what You tell me, especially in Your book, the Bible. In Jesus' name. Amen.

The Gift of Honor

"If I'm your Father, where's the honor?"
—MALACHI 1:6

There are two things that a good father needs to show: loving affection and loving authority. When this happens, he fosters two things: relationship and respect. According to the Bible, God is the perfect Father. He shows His affection and exercises His authority with perfect love. This means that we must not only relate to Him in an intimate way, we must also look up to Him with the honor that He deserves. This is the point that Malachi is making. God is our Father, but this does not mean that we can disrespect Him. Intimacy does not mean complacency. When a person comes to know God as their Father, they need to remember His authority as well as His affection. God is an awesome Father as well as a doting Father. We should not just relate to Him. We should always respect Him with honor.

PRAYER

Dear Father, help me to get the balance right in my love for You. Teach me to cultivate both relationship and respect. In Jesus' name. Amen.

Rebelling Against Love

"I imagined that you would say, 'Dear Father!'"
—JEREMIAH 3:19

In the last devotion we saw how there are verses about God as Father in the Old Testament. If that is so, then why did Jesus have to come at all? The answer is: because the children of Israel chose to walk away from the privilege of knowing God as their Dearest Father. God had offered them this great honor. As He says here, "I dreamed that you would say, 'Dear Father!'" The problem was that His people chose to pour out their affections upon false gods rather than on Him. In the end, this unfaithfulness led to disaster. It led to the Jewish people being sent into exile in Babylon 600 years before Jesus came. Although they returned to Judah, the reason why the Father had to send His Son was so that Jesus would do what Israel was called to do—to know the Father's love and share that love with the nations. Thank God for Jesus, who helps us to say, "Dear Father!"

PRAYER

Dear Father, help me always to set my affections on You, not on earthly idols. I choose to call You my "Dear Father" and to put You first. In Jesus' name. Amen.

You've Got a Nerve!

"You have the nerve to call out, 'My Father!'"
—JEREMIAH 3:4

Jeremiah is lamenting the fact that God's people are sinning by soliciting other gods. In response, God has stopped the rain, causing a drought. However, God's people are not fazed by this. They carry on sinning non-stop while praying, "My Father! You took care of me when I was a child. Why not now?" This is a serious mistake and yet it is amazing how many still make it, even to this day. There are far too many who call God "my Father," "my Dad," "my Papa," and yet who keep sinning. Why is this? It is because we have embraced a false belief that it's alright to go on sinning because Father will simply go on forgiving us, as He's done before. This is a very dangerous view, as Israel's history warns us. Having the nerve to call God "My Father" while living in constant sin will always end in disaster.

PRAYER

Help me, my Father, to live like a true son, a true daughter, and to imitate Jesus, who resisted sin throughout His life. In His name. Amen.

Family Unity

> Don't we all come from one Father? Aren't we all
> created by the same God? So why can't we get along?
> −MALACHI 2:10

When we are out of sync with the Father's love, it's not long before we find that we are out of sync with each other. When we allow sin to separate us from the Father's love, it isn't long before our human relationships suffer too. This is precisely what happened in Malachi's day. The priests had disobeyed God. They had broken their covenant with the Father. Malachi sees the devastating consequences in the breakdown of unity among God's family. He implores them to remember that they are all children of the same Father and to restore their love for God and in the process get along with each other. Let's seek to strengthen our love for the Father so that we will always enjoy harmony in our relationships with others in our family and in the family of God.

PRAYER

*Dear Father, help me to love You with such a
faithfulness and affection that all my earthly
relationships will be strengthened. In Jesus'
name. Amen.*

Heavenly Heart Bursts

> "Oh! Ephraim is my dear, dear son,
> my child in whom I take pleasure!
> Every time I mention his name,
> my heart bursts with longing for him!
> Everything in me cries out for him.
> Softly and tenderly I wait for him."
> —JEREMIAH 31:20

If we want to go deeper into the Father's heart, there are few verses more revealing than this. The Jewish people are in exile in Babylon. They weep with homesick longing for the city of Jerusalem. What is the Father doing? This verse tells us. He remembers His dear, dear son, Israel (here called "Ephraim"). His heart, overflowing with fatherly affection, cries out for the child that brings Him such joy. Above all, He waits for His son to return to Him. What a beautiful picture this is of the Father's heart. When we fall or fail, our Father doesn't turn His back on us. His heart bursts with love as He waits for us to come on home.

PRAYER

Dear Father, I thank You for softly and tenderly waiting for me when I let You down. You are the perfect Father and I give You praise. In Jesus' name. Amen.

Father of Eternity

His names will be: Amazing Counselor, Strong
God, Eternal Father, Prince of Wholeness.
—ISAIAH 9:6

The prophet Isaiah sees something in a vision. One day, there will be a son born on planet earth and He will come from King David's throne. This Son will have four names. One of these is "Eternal Father." The word in Hebrew is *Abiad,* a combination of *Abi* (Father) and *ad* (Eternity). What Isaiah foresaw was the coming of Jesus, who was not only to be Israel's Messiah, but also the Savior of the World. Jesus, as the Father's Son, would be so close to the Father's heart that He would be able to say to His followers, "If you've seen me, you've seen the Father." Jesus is the complete and infallible revelation of the Father of Eternity. He is the Amazing Counselor, Strong God and Prince of Wholeness too. The baby who will be born in a manger is accordingly an eternal being. In Bethlehem, the infinite will become an infant!

PRAYER

Thank You, Jesus, for stepping down from Heaven and revealing the Father of Eternity. Help me to enjoy the wholeness of Your love. In Your name. Amen.

His Happy Thoughts

He'll calm you with His love
and delight you with His songs.
—ZEPHANIAH 3:17

Here Zephaniah foresees a day of great restoration for God's people. One day the Father will calm their troubled hearts and bring delight to their homesick souls with His songs of joy. What a beautiful picture this is of the Father's love! When we return to Him and live in obedience to His ways, He takes us in His arms and speaks peace to our restless souls. In His enfolding embrace, there is a deep serenity that the world can never give. But there's more! When we position ourselves like this before God, He rejoices over us with singing. He causes pleasure to combine with peace as we hear His singing over us. When we are walking in His ways, we are the Father's happy thoughts. We bring Him such pleasure that He jumps up and down with joy in Heaven and sings with uninhibited delight.

PRAYER

Father, I choose out of love to live according to Your will, Your Word, and Your ways, so that I may consistently be Your happy thought. In Jesus' name. Amen.

A Future Hope

I have it all planned out—plans to take
care of you, not abandon you, plans to
give you the future you hope for.
—JEREMIAH 29:11

We have seen the Father's heart for Israel in many different ways in these devotions. We have seen how the Father adopted Israel out of all the nations of the earth. We have seen how He took Israel by the hand and trained him in the way he should go. We have seen how He rebuked Israel when he was disobedient and restored Israel when he was sorry. Now this son called Israel is in exile in Babylon, far from home. He is weeping with regret. Into that situation, Jeremiah says something like this: "The Father still loves you. He plans to take care of you and will not abandon you. He has a plan to fulfill your desires and to give you a good future." What a good, good Father! What He promised to the Jewish people, He promises to us as well. Let's never lose hope. Father God has a good plan for our lives!

PRAYER

Dear Father, thank You that You have a plan to prosper, not to harm me, a plan that gives me a hope and a future. In Jesus' name. Amen.

Famous Last Words

He will turn the hearts of the fathers to the children,
and the hearts of the children to their fathers.
—MALACHI 4:6 (NKJV)

It would be tempting to feel that the Old Testament ends on a rather hopeless note with Israel separated from the Father. In a sense this is true. God offered Israel the opportunity of being His children. God had adopted Israel, yet Israel had rebelled against His love. However, this is not the end of the story. The Old Testament closes with a promise that in the future the fathers' hearts will be turned toward the hearts of their children, and the children's hearts turned toward their fathers. That promise was at last fulfilled when the Son of God was born. Now reconciliation would be possible at two levels. First of all, estranged spiritual orphans would find their way back to the Father's heart. Secondly, children estranged from their earthly fathers would find their way back into their fathers' arms. This is good news indeed! Through His life, death, and resurrection, Jesus was going to make it possible for us to turn our hearts back toward the Father and to be reunited. What's more, it would now be possible for earthly fathers and their children to experience reconciliation too!

PRAYER

Thank You, oh my Father, for giving us Your Son, so that we might turn our hearts to You, just as You have turned Your heart to us. In Jesus' name. Amen.

The Father Who Speaks

The Word was first.
—JOHN 1:1

Throughout the Old Testament, the Father had frequently spoken to His people through the prophets. These prophets were people who lived close to His heart and who heard His voice. The last words of the Old Testament, as we saw in the last devotion, were spoken by such a man. Malachi foresaw a time when there would be a miraculous reconciliation between fathers and their estranged children—a promise that applies to all human beings, separated as we are by sin from our Father in Heaven. The one who brings an end to the alienation between us and our Father is Jesus. Here, at the very start of his Gospel, John describes Jesus as "the Word." Whatever else this means, it means that we have a Father in Heaven who speaks. He is not a silent dad, emotionally or physically remote. No, He has consistently spoken through His prophets and now speaks with finality and fullness through His one and only Son. This Son, unlike the prophets, was alive before time began. This Son was present to the Father before the creation of the world. Aren't you grateful that we have a Father who speaks to us?

PRAYER

Dearest Father, I can't thank You enough that You spoke through the prophets but now supremely and completely through Your Son. Amen.

Always Present

The Word present to God.
—JOHN 1:2

At the very beginning of all things, Jesus was present to His Father and His Father was present to Him. Here we see a glimpse of the matchless love that exists between the Son and the Father in eternity. In Heaven, the Father was and is always present to His Son and the Son is always present to His Father. They enjoyed and enjoy forever face-to-face intimacy with each other. This is a window onto the love that forever flows in the Holy Spirit between the Father and the Son. Here on earth, fathers are not always present to their children, either emotionally or physically, so these children are not able to be present to their fathers. This is often a source of agony to children, who simply want their dads to enjoy hanging out with them. How different it is in Heaven. The Son loves being with His Father because the Father loves being with His Son. This is good news for us too. In Jesus Christ, we get to be present to the Father who loves being present to His children.

PRAYER

Dearest Father, help me to live like Jesus and to delight to be present to You every day, even as You delight to be present to me. Amen.

God With Skin

The Word was God,
in readiness for God from day one.
—JOHN 1:2

Jesus was not merely a wonderful human being, a great teacher, a mighty prophet. Jesus of Nazareth was and is the Word of God. Not only was this Word present with God before the world was made. This Word *was* God. How could Jesus be both with God and the same as God? No amount of ink has been spared when it comes to this. What we can say is this, the Son is one in being with the Father, while at the same time being an individual person, separate from the Father. The Son was poised, ready to do the Father's bidding from the very beginning, because He always delights to do the Father's will. When the Father was ready to respond to the cries of this alienated planet, the Son said, "I'll go." When the Father's heart broke over the barrier of sin between us and Him, the Son said, "I'll deal with it; I'll pay the price." Jesus' birth in a manger in Bethlehem is therefore a history-making moment. It is the arrival of the Word-made-flesh. In the baby Jesus we see the human face of Jehovah God.

PRAYER

Thank You, Jesus, that You are so much more than a great teacher or prophet. You are God with human skin; You are the Word made flesh. Amen.

Created in Love

*Everything was created through Him;
nothing—not one thing!—
came into being without Him.*
—JOHN 1:3

When God the Father created all things, He did so through the Word. Every time He acted, the Bible says, "And God said...." Since the beginning of the Church, people have understood this to be a reference to the activity of the Son of God, because He is the Word. What could be clearer? The Father created all things through His Word, i.e. through His Son. More than that, we can see that the Holy Spirit was involved too. He brooded over the formless void like a great bird, His wings spread over chaos, poised to bring life. So the creation of the heavens and the earth, as well as the creation of the first human beings, was a great collaboration between the three persons of the Trinity. Everything was created by the Father, through Jesus, with the help of the Holy Spirit. We were created by love, in love, and for love. Let's never forget: there is not a single thing that didn't come into existence without Jesus!

PRAYER

Dearest Father, I worship You for Your awesome creativity. Thank You for creating me by love, in love, and for love, and doing it all through Jesus. Amen.

The Life-Giving Father

What came into existence was Life,
and the Life was Light to live by.
—JOHN 1:4

Through Jesus, our Father in Heaven brought life and light to all things. This is a glorious truth. When we get to know Jesus, He introduces us to His Father. This is because He is the only Way to the Father, the only One who tells us the Truth about the Father, the only One who gives us the greatest gift of all—the Father's life. There is something infinitely special about this life. This life does not refer simply to our human existence. The life that comes from Abba Father is eternal, abundant, infinite, spiritual life. It is the kind of life that is enjoyed forever in Heaven—exhilarating and endless. When we come to know Jesus, this life flows from the Father, through Jesus, with the help of the Holy Spirit, into the deepest places of our lives. It floods the reservoirs of our spirits like a great light, bringing an end to the darkness, transforming us from death to eternal life. This Life is the Light to live by, and it is the Father's lavish gift.

PRAYER

*Dearest Father, thank You so much that through Jesus
You fill us with the never-ending and abundant life
and light of Heaven. In Your name. Amen.*

A Never-Ending Light

The Life-Light blazed out of the darkness;
the darkness couldn't put it out.
—JOHN 1:5

Before Jesus Christ was born, two thousand years ago, the world was filled with death and darkness. The sin of our first parents had brought separation from our Father in Heaven. Consequently, every person born on planet earth is a spiritual orphan, condemned to live in darkness and die in their sins. Then the Father said, "Enough is enough!" He sent His one and only Son, Jesus Christ, into this orphaned planet. This Son, the infinite Word of God, was born as an infant. He grew up to be a man without sin, to die upon the Cross for our sins. As a result, we who were spiritual orphans can now become the adopted children of God. This is a great honor and an indescribable joy. If we say "yes" to the invitation to follow Jesus, we are no longer dead in our sins but filled with the Father's life. More than that, we no longer live in darkness because this Life-Light blazes with an unquenchable fire. The devil can never put it out! Let's make sure that the unconquerable light of the Father's life is always burning in our hearts!

PRAYER

Dearest Father, thank You that Your light shines in the
darkness and the darkness can never put it out. May I
always be ablaze with Your love. Amen.

Here Comes the Son

The Word became flesh and blood,
and moved into the neighborhood.
—JOHN 1:14

Cometh the hour, cometh the man—and the man's name is Jesus! Here, at the beginning of John's Gospel, we hear about the birth of Jesus Christ. The Word of God moves into the neighborhood. In the original Greek, it says that He pitched His tent with us. We were alone in the desert of our orphaned existence, far away from God because of our sins, thirsty for His love, starved of all purpose. Then Jesus, the one and only Son of the Father, came and set up a tent in our wilderness. The one-of-a-kind Son of God took on human flesh when He was born as a baby. Here, at last, was the Father's answer to the separation between Himself and humanity. Abba Father could not tolerate our alienation any longer. The Son of God became a son of man so that the children of men might become the sons and daughters of God. What a history-making moment this was! When the infinite became an infant, the Father's love entered the world in Jesus. Our orphan state has ended and we can enjoy the presence of God in our own neighborhood!

PRAYER

Father God, thank You so much for sending Your only Son to end our orphan state and to deal so decisively with our alienation from You. Amen.

The Tent of Glory

We saw the glory with our own eyes, the one-of-a-
kind glory, like Father, like Son.
—John 1:14

When John (who wrote these words) talked about Jesus, He talked about "glory." Glory here does not refer to the kind of adulation afforded to celebrities today in the media. No, glory here refers to the radiant glory of the presence of God. It refers to the heavy weight of the light-filled majesty of Almighty God. In Jesus of Nazareth, John says that "we" saw this glory, referring to himself and the other eyewitnesses of Jesus. Keep in mind that John has just said that Jesus "pitched His tent" among us. In the time of Moses, a tent was set up in the wilderness. This Tabernacle became the place where the glory of God rested in the Holy of Holies. The *shekinah* (glory of God) dwelled in a *mishkan* (tent). What John is saying here is extraordinary: "The majestic glory of the Father's presence no longer resides in a tent. It resides in the body of Jesus. And we have seen that glorious presence with our own eyes—the one-of-a-kind majesty of the Father, pouring out of the Son!" Let's never forget: Jesus of Nazareth was the tent in which the Father's glory dwelled!

PRAYER

Lord Jesus, I give You the highest praise because You
pitched Your tent among us and became the human
habitation for the Father's glory. Amen.

Grace and Truth

Generous inside and out,
true from start to finish.
—JOHN 1:14

John is still singing the praises of Jesus at the beginning of his Gospel, and we are camping out for a while with him, joining in with his adoration. John has just celebrated the fact that Jesus pitched His tent among us and rejoiced that this tent (Jesus' body) was filled with the presence of the glory of God, just as the Tabernacle of Moses was. Now John says something more: Jesus embodied and displayed two of the Father's greatest virtues: grace and truth. Grace here is the same as the Old Testament Hebrew word often translated "mercy" (*hesed*). Truth corresponds to the word "faithfulness" (*hemet*). Ever since the beginning, our Father in Heaven has displayed mercy toward His people and faithfulness to His covenant. He has been generous and kind and He has been faithful and true. Now, in Jesus Christ, we see the Father's attributes on display. From the beginning of His life to its end, Jesus showcased the undeserved mercy and loving faithfulness of our Father in Heaven. Doesn't that make you want to give Him the highest praise?

PRAYER

Dear Lord Jesus, I thank You that You manifested the Father's generous compassion and His steadfast love, and that You still do today. Amen.

The Gift Giver

We all live off his generous bounty,
gift after gift after gift.
—JOHN 1:16

This is a glorious encouragement! When Jesus Christ was born, He began to fill the world with the Father's blessings. Yes, I said "blessings" plural. Anyone who comes to know Jesus Christ—who repents of their sins and puts their trust in Him—becomes a recipient of the Father's lavish generosity. In Jesus Christ, we get to receive one blessing after another. This can be hard to believe if you've had a father who was stingy. You may find it difficult to trust that God is a Father who gives us gift after gift. But this is exactly what our Heavenly Father is like. He is not like earthly fathers, even the best of them. He gives gifts that have eternal significance. He gave us the gift of His Son. He gave us the gift of salvation. He gave us the gift of the Spirit—and indeed the gifts of the Spirit too. This Father is full of generous bounty and He wants to lavish His endless generosity on us as His children. Let's not project the face of mean fathers onto God. Let's enjoy the extravagant love of the Father.

PRAYER

Dearest Father, I thank You that You are not a miserly dad but the most generous Father of all. Help me to live off Your generous bounty. Amen.

Children of the Father

> But whoever did want him,
> who believed he was who he claimed
> and would do what he said,
> he made to be their true selves,
> their child-of-God selves.
> —JOHN 1:12

Ever since Jesus began His ministry on earth, this one simple fact has been true: many have rejected Him while some have accepted Him. The same is still true today. Those who accept Jesus do so because they believe (and go on believing) that Jesus is exactly who He claimed to be—the one and only Son of the Father. Whenever a person does that, they become a child of God. They become who they were truly created to be and they embrace their real identity—"their child-of-God selves." This is what the Father is looking for—people who will believe in His Son, Jesus Christ. To those people He gives the right to become His son or daughter, representing the Father on earth, bringing the powerful presence of the Father's love to those around us.

PRAYER

Jesus, I believe that You are the Son of God, and that thanks to what You did two thousand years ago, I am a child of my Father. In Your name. Amen.

Who's the Dad?

"Joseph, son of David, don't hesitate to get
married. Mary's pregnancy is Spirit-conceived.
God's Holy Spirit has made her pregnant."
—MATTHEW 1:20

In the run-up to Jesus' birth, things did not proceed without complications. Joseph was betrothed to Mary and was waiting for that happy day when he could return to Mary's home and take her to his house to be his bride. On that day there would be great celebrations. However, in the months leading up to it, Joseph learned that Mary had become pregnant. According to the law, he had every right to divorce her, which he resolved to do quietly, to protect her honor. However, an angel told Joseph not to do this because it was not by another man but by the Holy Spirit that Mary was now pregnant. Hearing this, Joseph did everything the angel commanded and married Mary. From that day on, Joseph knew that even though Mary was the child's mother, he was not his true father. We should never forget that God Almighty is the Father of Jesus of Nazareth. Although He had a human mother, He had and has forever a divine Father.

PRAYER

*I praise You, Jesus, because You are utterly unique in
Your conception, because it was by the Holy Spirit You
became a human being. Amen.*

A Stepfather's Love

Joseph obeyed.
—MATTHEW 2:21

When Joseph married Mary, it wasn't long before he helped her to give birth to a son that was not his own. We should never forget this. Joseph was effectively a stepfather to Jesus. Even though Jesus was not his boy, he cared for Him as if He was. What an amazing father figure Joseph is, and what a great example to all substitute fathers. All over the world there are men who are stepfathers, surrogate fathers, stand-in fathers, spiritual fathers, adoptive fathers, and foster fathers. These are men, like Joseph, who have taken on the responsibility to show a fatherly love to children who would otherwise be fatherless. Let's champion Joseph a bit more when we celebrate the story of Jesus' birth and infancy. He was not a redundant figure in Jesus' early years. He was an essential mentor, not only in the home, but in the carpentry shop as well. Above all, he was an example of a man who obeyed God whenever God told him to do something. Stand-in fathers like Joseph sometimes reveal more of the Father's heart than even biological fathers do.

PRAYER

Thank You, Heavenly Father, for the example of Joseph, who reveals Your tender heart toward those without a father. In Jesus' name. Amen.

The Dreaming Dad

Joseph was directed in a dream to
go to the hills of Galilee.
—MATTHEW 2:22

There are two famous men in the Bible called Joseph. The first was one of the sons of Jacob, who went on to become a ruler in the court of Pharaoh in Egypt. The second was the stepfather of Jesus. What both of these men had in common is the fact that God spoke to them in dreams. This is especially evident in the story of Jesus' birth and infancy. Here we see Joseph, the stepfather of Jesus, being constantly guided by God in dreams. It is in a dream that Joseph learns that Mary is pregnant by the Holy Spirit. It is in a dream that Joseph is warned to take Mary and Jesus to Egypt. It is in a dream that Joseph is told to take Mary and Jesus back from Egypt to Israel. It is in a dream that Joseph is given the exact address—the hill country of Galilee and the town of Nazareth. What a great example it was for Jesus to be mentored by a father who was prepared to be directed at every step by His Heavenly Father.

PRAYER

Father, teach me how to be more like Joseph and to live in a constant openness to Your guidance and obedience to Your direction. In Jesus' name. Amen.

A Father's Blessing

"And you, my child, 'Prophet of the Highest'
will go ahead of the Master to prepare his ways."
—LUKE 1:76

Another father who features in Jesus' infancy is a man called Zechariah. He was the father of John the Baptist. He was in his sixties when an angel appeared to him as he was serving as a priest in the Temple in Jerusalem. This angel told him that his wife Elizabeth was going to have a baby. Zechariah's reply was effectively, "I don't believe it!" For that he was struck dumb for nine months until his child was born. Then, at last, his speech was restored. What did he say? After naming the child John (who would become John the Baptist, the forerunner of Jesus), Zechariah began to utter the most extraordinary blessing over his newborn. In the middle of that blessing he began to speak prophetic words of destiny, telling his baby that he would be the Prophet of the Most High God and that he would prepare the way for the Lord. What a wonderful thing it is when fathers speak words of blessing and hope over their children. When they do this, they put on display our Heavenly Father's heart.

PRAYER

Dear Father, please teach fathers how to do what You do—to bless children with words that give a hope and a future. In Jesus' name. Amen.

As Plain as Day

This one-of-a-kind God-Expression,
who exists at the very heart of the Father,
has made him plain as day.
—JOHN 1:18

There are three things to celebrate here. The first is that Jesus is "one of a kind." He is the one and only Son of God by nature. We are sons and daughters *by adoption*; He is Son *by nature*. Secondly, He lives forever at the Father's heart. When He was on earth, Jesus enjoyed the closest communion with His *Abba* in Heaven. Now, having died and risen again, He has returned to the throne of God and forever rests upon His Father. Thirdly, this same Jesus came into the world and taught us all about the Father. In fact, through everything He said and everything He did, Jesus made it "plain as day" what our Father God is really like. Thank God for Jesus. Give Jesus all the praise for being one of a kind, for His intimacy with the Father, and for giving us such a clear picture of the world's greatest Dad.

PRAYER

Dear Lord Jesus, I give You the highest praise for being the one and only Son of God and for showing us what the Father's heart is truly like. Amen.

The Son's Mission

"No one has seen the Father except the One
who has his Being alongside the Father."
—John 6:46

Jesus is one of a kind. He alone is the Son of God, and the call upon our lives is to come to a place where we truly believe this. Jesus Christ came from Heaven to earth to reveal what the Father is like and to die upon the Cross so that we might be reconciled to the Father. Jesus could do this because He shares the same nature as the Father. Even though He was fully human on the earth, He was also at the same time fully divine. Only someone who was both God and man could bridge the gap between man and God. We must, therefore, never forget that Jesus is the only Son *by nature,* while we are sons and daughters of God *by adoption.* Jesus alone has seen the Father face to face. He came to this earth to show us the Father. Without Him, we would never have truly known what the Father is like.

PRAYER

*Dear Lord Jesus, I worship You for being one of a kind.
I believe that You truly are the unique Son of God. In
Your name. Amen.*

A Lost Boy

> "Young man, why have you done this to
> us? Your father and I have been half out
> of our minds looking for you."
> —LUKE 2:48

Have you ever lost a child in a crowded street or on a walk in the park? In the last year of His childhood, aged 12, Jesus goes missing in Jerusalem when His family go up to the city. They are halfway home before Mary realizes that He's not with Joseph, and Joseph realizes that He's not with Mary. Clearly they were in the equivalent of a wagon train. When Mary and Joseph eventually find Him, He's in the Temple precincts engaged in theological discussions with the top religious thinkers of the day! Their first words to Jesus are not, "You're a clever boy, outwitting the scholars." It's, "We were half out of our minds searching for you." Let's never forget that Jesus had a stepfather who experienced the agony of losing his son, even just for a few hours. In this he learned something profound about the Father, who never stops seeking the lost.

PRAYER

Thank You, Father, that You are passionate about pursuing Your lost children on the earth. Thank You that Your love never fails and never gives up. Amen.

My Father's Things

"Didn't you know that I had to be here,
dealing with the things of my Father?"
—LUKE 2:49

Jesus' childhood ended at the age of 13 when He had His Bar Mitzvah. This was when His life as an adult began. Up until the age of 13, Jesus must have had a growing intimation in His human heart that God was His Father and that He was His much loved, only Son. We have some evidence of this because by the age of 12, toward the end of His childhood, Jesus was calling God "my Father." This is clear from the verse above where Jesus replies to His exasperated parents who had lost Him during a journey from Jerusalem. On the way back, Jesus' parents realize that He isn't with them! When they find Him in the Temple and ask Him what He has been doing, Jesus replies to them. "Did you not know I had to be about my Father's things?" Jesus understood, even as a child, that His greatest priority in life was to put His Father's things first. What would happen today if all over the world children and young people resolved to put first "their Father's things"? There would be global revival!

PRAYER

*Help us, dear Lord Jesus, to bring up our children to
know the Father intimately and to put His things first
in their lives. In Your name. Amen.*

Abba Father

"My Father."
—LUKE 2:49

In the previous devotion we saw how Jesus told His parents that He was about "the things of my Father." Let's look at the words "My Father." Jesus spoke Aramaic. In that language the word we translate "Father" is *Abba*. What does this mean? Not long ago I was asked to speak in Israel about the Father's love. I stayed with an Israeli family who spoke in Hebrew. They had all come to faith in Jesus. During the week I saw children climb all over their father when he came from work. As they did, they shouted out, "Abba!" I asked the father what the significance of this word was. He replied firmly, "It's intimate!" Isn't it an amazing thing that Jesus referred to God in this way from a very early age? Unlike so many others in His day, who talked to God as if He was a remote deity, Jesus talked to Him as a relational Daddy. Let's never forget how radical Jesus is. When He revealed God to us, He showed that God is intimate!

PRAYER

Dear Lord Jesus, help me by Your Holy Spirit to know God as my relational and intimate Daddy, not as a remote deity. In Your name. Amen.

Pride and Joy

"You are my Son, chosen and marked
by my love, pride of my life."
—MARK 1:11

After 30 years living in anonymity in Nazareth, Jesus emerged on the stage of history to declare that God is our Father and that the Kingdom of Heaven had come on the earth. When did this transition from invisibility to visibility take place? It occurred when Jesus was baptized in the Jordan. This was a moment of monumental significance. When Jesus came out of the water He heard the voice of His Heavenly Father saying: "You are my Son." Was this some kind of adoption? No, this was an affirmation of what Jesus already knew: that God was His loving Father and that He was the Father's only Son. That reaffirmation was a crucial prelude to the beginning of Jesus' public ministry. When Jesus heard His Father call Him "chosen" and "marked by my love," the Father's affection overwhelmed Him. When He heard His Father saying, "You're the pride of my life," He received the Father's seal of approval. As God's adopted daughters and sons, let's resolve every day to live under an open Heaven and hear our Father say, "You're the pride of my life!"

PRAYER

Thank You Jesus, for becoming flesh and living as a man so that we could know God as an affectionate, accepting and affirming Father. In Your name. Amen.

The Dove of Heaven

After all the people were baptized, Jesus was baptized.
As he was praying, the sky opened up and the Holy
Spirit, like a dove descending, came down on him.
—LUKE 3:21–22

With the baptism of Jesus, history has been given a new start. This is evident from the descent of the Holy Spirit "like a dove." When God created the earth, the Holy Spirit brooded over the chaos like a great bird. When God gave the earth a new beginning in the time of Noah, the fresh start was signaled by the arrival of a dove. When Jesus was baptized, the Holy Spirit came upon Jesus like a dove, marking a fresh new beginning in human history. What went on in Jesus' heart as the Spirit touched His life? What did Jesus experience as He was touched by the dove of Heaven? The answer is: He was embraced by the Father's affection in a way that was unparalleled in His human life thus far. This marked a new beginning for Him—the birth of His public ministry. It marked a new beginning for all of us—the beginning of a new age in which we can now call God our Father. This is a lasting lesson—we cannot be touched by the love of Heaven without the dove of Heaven!

PRAYER

Dear Father, I ask that You would give me a baptismal experience of being overwhelmed by Your heavenly love, just as You did with Jesus. Amen.

Word and Spirit

And along with the Spirit, a voice: "You are my Son,
chosen and marked by my love, pride of my life."
—LUKE 3:22

How is a person today to know the Father's love in their hearts? Jesus' baptism gives us the answer. There are two things we need. The first is the Holy Spirit. When Jesus was baptized in the Father's love, it was through the Holy Spirit. Jesus felt something in His human heart—the captivating and unconditional acceptance of His Father's love. But then there's a second thing we need. Luke says that, along with the Holy Spirit Jesus heard His Father's voice. If you look carefully, you'll see that what the Father said from Heaven was actually made up of phrases from the Book of Psalms and the Book of Isaiah, and other Scriptures too. When the Father affirmed His Son, He did so using His book—the Bible. This is an important reminder. No one will really experience the Father's love unless they live in both the Word and the Spirit. When we hear the Father's voice through His Word, and receive His touch by His Spirit, then we will be overwhelmed by His love.

PRAYER

*Help me, dear Father, to know Your love through what
You have said in Your Word and through receiving
Your Spirit. In Jesus' name. Amen.*

Standing Firm

Next Jesus was taken into the wild by the Spirit
for the Test. The Devil was ready to give it.
—MATTHEW 4:1

Directly after His baptism Jesus encounters the devil's attack
in the desert. This is provides us with an important lesson. The
Father knew that His Son would be tempted but He made very
sure that His Son experienced His love before that happened.
How gracious is that! The same is true for us. The Father wants
His children to know without doubt that they are the adopted
sons and daughters of God, before the enemy tries to sow doubt
by saying, "If you are a son," "If you are a daughter." Once you
and I have been in the river with Jesus, believing by God's Word
that the Father loves us, knowing from His touch that He adores
us, then it doesn't matter what deserts we have to go through,
or what trials we have to face. We will never doubt that we are
God's beloved sons and daughters. The Father's love will be the
foundational reality in our lives. It is the bedrock of our hearts.
Consequently, we shall not be moved by the trials of life and the
temptations of the deceiver. We can stand up to the devil in the
desert and say, "It is written!"

PRAYER

*Dear Father, I pray in Jesus' name that You will help
me to be rooted and grounded in Your amazing love, so
that I can stand firm under any test. Amen.*

Working *From* Approval

> Jesus went to Galilee preaching the Message
> of God: "Time's up! God's kingdom is here.
> Change your life and believe the Message."
> —MARK 1:14–15

There are three stages to the start of Jesus' public ministry. There is first of all the baptism of Jesus, then the temptations in the desert, and finally, the launch of Jesus' ministry of proclamation and demonstration—preaching that the Kingdom of Heaven has arrived on the earth, and the evidence of that is the healing of the sick, the cleansing of lepers, the stilling of storms, the deliverance of the oppressed, and the raising of the dead. Please note that when the Father says to Jesus, "You're the pride of my life" at the baptism, Jesus hasn't done any of these things yet. Many of us have been used to dads who only told us they were proud of us when we achieved something. Not so with Abba Father; He affirms His Son because of His position, not His performance. This should be the default setting for us too. Let's rejoice in the fact that the Father loves us for who we are. Let's work *from* approval, not *for* approval.

PRAYER

*Lord Jesus, in a world where everyone is seeking to rest
from work, help me to work from rest—the rest that
comes from knowing the Father's love. Amen.*

Dad's Dreams

"Come with me. I'll make a new kind of
fisherman out of you. I'll show you how to catch
men and women instead of perch and bass."
—MARK 1:17

As Jesus begins His ministry, He calls the disciples to follow Him. He chooses 12 men in all because He wants to show that He is doing what Israel failed to do. Israel failed to walk in the Father's blessing and give it away to the nations. So Jesus selects 12 men in memory of the 12 tribes of Israel. To these men He not only gives the Father's blessing, but He also tasks them to take this blessing to the ends of the earth, just as God had promised Abraham in Genesis 12. The first three men he calls are Peter, James, and John. Jesus prophesies over them that they will no longer be catching fish; they will be catching men and women in the net of the Father's love. What a great promise! What a wonderful future! We have a good, good Father in Heaven who has an epic plan for our lives. When we choose to follow Jesus, we stop following our daydreams and we start pursuing our Dad's dreams!

PRAYER

*Thank You, my Father, that You have an awesome
dream for my life. Help me to align myself with Your
dream, not my own. In Jesus' name. Amen.*

The Greatest Teacher

> They were surprised at his teaching—so
> forthright, so confident—not quibbling
> and quoting like the religion scholars.
> —MARK 1:22

Jesus is by far and away the greatest teacher that has ever graced the stage of history. Why is that? It has to do with the practice of derivation. Even the best teachers tend to derive their insights from other people. They spend many years studying other books and listening to other educators, and they shape their views using those sources. Not so Jesus. Jesus derived His insights, not from books and scholars, but from His Father in Heaven. This is why His contemporaries were so awestruck by His teaching. He didn't get His thoughts from earth, but from Heaven. He didn't get it from the fathers of His tradition, but from His Father in Heaven. In other words, His insights came from intimacy—intimacy with His Father. Jesus' public ministry of preaching and teaching was remarkable for many reasons, but most of all because of His practice of derivation—His truths arose from revelation, not research. They came from the Father's heart, not from men's books.

PRAYER

Dear Father, help me to cultivate my intimacy with
You so that I may always communicate the wisdom of
Heaven in every situation. In Jesus' name. Amen.

Intimacy and Insight

"I have it firsthand from the Father."
—JOHN 6:45

Everyone else in Jesus' day received knowledge about God secondhand, as it were. They relied on the teaching and traditions of others. With Jesus, however, it was altogether different. He received everything directly from His Father. He did not get it out of books or from the latest teachings of the rabbis. He received it by revelation from the Father. Out of great intimacy flowed unique insights. This is why others went around talking about God as *Adonai* ("Lord") while Jesus talked about God as *Abba* ("Papa"). Yes, Jesus knew that God is Lord, but He also knew that God is supremely our Father. This is why so many people in His day reacted with wonder whenever Jesus opened His mouth. They knew that while others derived their knowledge from tradition, Jesus received His by revelation. What an example Jesus has set for us! We too can know Papa this intimately and share the Father's love with others.

PRAYER

Dear Lord Jesus, thank You for showing us that intimacy with the Father is what we need to bring life to those around us. In Your name. Amen.

Actions Speak Louder

> "What's going on here? A new teaching
> that does what it says? He shuts up defiling,
> demonic spirits and sends them packing!"
> —MARK 1:27

In the last devotion we saw one of the reasons why Jesus' preaching and teaching was so different—He derived His insights directly from His Father. But there is a second reason and this has to do with the practice of demonstration. Jesus not only taught that Heaven had come on earth, He also proved it by setting the captives free. In other words, He backed up the proclamation with a demonstration. He supplied "a new teaching that does what it says." Here again we see the Father's heart. We do not have a father who says He's going to do something but then doesn't back that up with actions. We have a Father who backs up His message with miracles! This was at the very heart of Jesus' unique ministry—He talked about the Father's love in an unprecedented way and He demonstrated that love with mighty works.

PRAYER

*Father, I want to represent Your love, not only with
Your wisdom, but also with Your power, just as Jesus
did. Help me to be more like Your Son. Amen.*

The Untouchables

A leper came to Him, begging on his knees,
"If you want to, you can cleanse me."
—MARK 1:40

Throughout His earthly ministry, Jesus demonstrated the Father's love in so many different ways. One of the most startling ways was in His treatment of those whom His contemporaries shunned and ostracized—the lepers. Keep in mind that in the Old Testament era, the clean person was terrified of being made unclean by leprosy. In Jesus we see the opposite. It's no longer the unclean infecting the clean; it's the clean infecting the unclean! Jesus doesn't worry about being made unclean by the leper. The leper is now the one in danger of being infected by the clean man! This is so radical and so counterintuitive. This is the culture of Heaven we're watching, where the Father's love extends with revolutionary kindness toward the unloved, where the Father's hand reaches out to touch and transform the untouchable ones! Don't you just love the way Jesus reveals the Father's heart! Let's touch everyone with the Father's infectious love!

PRAYER

Dear Father, thank You that in the Kingdom of Heaven we see Your radical love so clearly. Help me to start a revolution of kindness in my world. Amen.

Alone With Father

As often as possible Jesus withdrew to
out-of-the-way places for prayer.
—LUKE 5:16

It is so important to realize that Jesus not only engaged in public ministry, but He also spent times alone in prayer. We need to understand that when it comes to the Father's love, the public is an expression and extension of the private. In other words, the more we seek to encounter the Father's love in the private place, the more we will display the Father's love in the public sphere. If Jesus, as the one and only Son of God by nature, needed to spend time alone with His Father, then how much more do we, as the adopted sons and daughters of God? This is the secret to Jesus' ministry—a healthy rhythm of life in which solitary times with the Father in private resourced the public ministry of demonstrating that love. Everything Jesus needed for the public realm was supplied to Him in the secret place, as He communed with His Papa. This is the rhythm of life we need to embrace too.

PRAYER

Dearest Father, help me to be more like Your
Son, seeking Your face in the private place before
demonstrating Your love in the public space. Amen.

Complete Dependence

"The Son can't independently do a thing,
only what he sees the Father doing."
—JOHN 5:19

What a great example Jesus is! He did not act independently in His public ministry. At every moment He was entirely dependent upon His Father. This is true humility. If pride is acting independently of God and relying on our own resources, then humility means abandoning ourselves in total surrender to God's Word, His will and His ways. In this respect, Jesus not only shows us what the Father is like, but He also shows us what a true son or a daughter is like. If you and I want to be like Jesus, then we need to make it our highest aim every day to do only what we see our Father doing. The number-one priority is not to ask the Father to bless what we are doing but rather to find what *Abba* is doing and bless that. This is how Jesus lived. This is how a good daughter or son lives too!

PRAYER

*Dear Jesus, thank You for showing us the importance of
doing only what we see Abba Father doing. Help us to
learn how to do this. In Your name. Amen.*

Imitating Papa

"What the Father does, the Son does."
—JOHN 5;19

What went through Jesus' mind each day? This verse tells us. He sought to discover by the Holy Spirit what His Father was doing. This meant that every day was an adventure. One day Jesus saw His Father turning water into wine, so that's what He did. The next day He saw His Father cleansing a leper, so that's what He did too. Our lives are lived from a very different perspective. We do what we need to do and we ask the Father to bless that. Jesus shows us a very different way of living—the importance of abiding so close to the Father's heart that we know by the Holy Spirit what He is doing and we see what our Papa is doing and do that instead. What would happen if all the royally adopted sons and daughters of God decided to live this way? There would be Heaven on earth!

PRAYER

Jesus, help me to stop asking the Father to bless what I am doing and to start seeing what the Father is doing and to do that. In Your name. Amen.

The Run of the House

"A slave is a transient, who can't come and go
at will. The Son, though, has an established
position, the run of the house."
—JOHN 8:35

There are two sorts of people in the world—there are slaves
and there are sons (this includes daughters). Slaves come in two
shapes. The first is the slave to sin. The second is the slave to
law. The slave to sin is someone who is enticed, then entrapped,
before finally being enslaved. The slave to law strives constantly
to earn God's acceptance through observing every religious rule
and every religious ritual. In John chapter 8, Jesus tells the Jewish leaders that they are constantly slaving away in the hope that
the Father might one day love them. This is to survive rather than
thrive. It is bondage not freedom. Living as a son or a daughter
is the only alternative. The son is assured of a permanent place
in the Father's presence. Indeed, he has the run of the Father's
house! The one way a person can move from slavery to sonship is
by following Jesus. He alone sets the captives free.

PRAYER

*Dearest Father, please deliver me from being a slave to
sin or a slave to law. I don't want to be a transient slave;
I want to be a permanent son. Amen.*

The Two Fathers

"I'm talking about things I have seen while keeping
company with the Father, and you just go on
doing what you have heard from your father."
—JOHN 8:38

Jesus is having a heated debate with the Jewish leaders in Jerusalem. These are the people who are hell-bent on having Him killed. Jesus tells them that there are two fathers. The first is the Father of life—this is Jesus' Father. Then there is the father of lies—this is the devil that deceives people into becoming slaves. Jesus tells these religious authorities that everything he teaches has come directly from listening to His Father. This is the Father who longs to bring life to everyone, including them! They, on the other hand, know another father. They relate to the father of lies. This is why they cannot accept that Jesus is the Father's Son and the Savior of the World. They are in bondage to a demonic stronghold over their thinking—a mindset that says that only those who have Abraham as their father, and who keep the law to the letter, are accepted by God. Which father would you rather know?

PRAYER

*Lord Jesus, please deliver me from the father of lies and
help me always to keep company with the Father of
life—Your Father, and mine. In Your name. Amen.*

A Counterfeit Father

"You're from your father, the Devil, and
all you want to do is please him."
—JOHN 8:44

This is one of the hardest sayings of Jesus in the Gospels. The first thing we need to understand is this: Jesus is not describing the Jewish people in general. He is describing the Jewish leaders who refuse to see that they have had an opportunity to be set free by the Truth (that is, Jesus) but have said no. Those people—whatever race or background—show that they only want to please the father of lies. Secondly, we must remember that at the Cross, Jesus paid the price for us to be redeemed from slavery and adopted into sonship. Those who stay in a place of slavery—whether that's slavery to sin or slavery to law—show that they want to remain under the authority of the father of lies. As we saw in the previous devotion, there are really only two fathers. One brings life; the other—a counterfeit of true fatherhood—tells lies. Let's keep company with the Father of life and let's resist the father of lies who wants us to drift back into slavery, whatever form that may take.

PRAYER

*Dear Lord Jesus, I thank You that You are the truth
that sets me free. Help me always to walk in Your truth
and to reject the lies of the enemy. Amen.*

A Lifestyle of Honor

"I simply honor my Father."
—JOHN 8:49

To honor someone is to give them value. To shame someone is to communicate in words or actions that they have no worth at all. When it comes to our relationship with Abba Father, we must understand first of all that He has chosen to honor us. He has given us infinite value by calling us His beloved sons and daughters. What is the best response to this undeserved gift? It is to spend the rest of our lives giving honor to Him. We do this in two ways. First of all we live lives of worship. Worship has the word "worth" at the start. When we adore our Father, when we thank Him and give Him the highest praise, we are effectively saying, "You are worth more to me than anyone or anything." Secondly, we honor Abba Father in what we do. We make sure that our lives cause others to give our Father the value, esteem, worth and glory that He deserves. This is how Jesus lived, which is why He said, "I simply honor my Father." This is what we are called to do too.

PRAYER

Dearest Father, I want to live a life of beautiful simplicity in which I constantly declare Your worth in my words and in my deeds. In Jesus' name. Amen.

My Dad Is Stronger

"The Father who put them under my care is so
much greater than the Destroyer and Thief."
—JOHN 10:29

Jesus says that the devil is a thief who comes to steal, kill and
destroy, while He has come to give us life in all its fullness. Hearing this, it would be all too easy to think that we are caught in
the center of a spiritual battle between equals—Jesus on the
one hand, the devil on the other. This is not true. Jesus Christ is
greater, higher, mightier and stronger than the devil ever has been
or ever will be. This is why Jesus says that His Father is so much
greater than the one who tries to destroy and rob His followers.
Let's always remember this, especially when the enemy seems to
come into our lives like a flood. We need to lift up a standard that
declares, "My Dad is Stronger!" We need to remember that with
our Father's help we get to walk into the enemy's camp and take
back what the thief stole from us. If you are a follower of Jesus,
you're on the winning side!

PRAYER

*Dearest Father, I declare that You are greater, higher,
mightier and stronger than the devil has been or ever
will be, in Jesus' all-powerful name. Amen.*

Father's Orders

"The Father who sent me gave me orders,
told me what to say and how to say it."
—JOHN 12:49

Don't you just love the intimacy and unity that existed between Jesus and His Heavenly Father? Not only did Jesus depend on His Father when it came to the things He did (such as His miracles), but He also relied upon the Father when it came to the things He said. Notice something intriguing here: Jesus not only heard what the Father was saying, He also heard how to say it. That means that Jesus depended on His Father not only for the *content* of His words but also for the *form* too. One moment Jesus heard His Father speaking in parables, and the next in proverbs. One moment He heard Him speak in puns, and the next in preaching. What would it be like if we drew so close to the Father's heart that we said only what He was saying? I am guessing that we would listen more and speak less—that before we said anything, we would say quietly in our hearts, "Abba, show me what to say and how to say it."

PRAYER

Father, help me to cultivate a lifestyle of true sonship.
Teach me how to hear not only what You're saying, but
how You're saying it. In Jesus' name. Amen.

A Radical Revelation

"Our Father in heaven."
—MATTHEW 6:9

Sometimes familiarity can cause indifference. This is true in the case of the Lord's Prayer. This is the prayer that Jesus taught His followers, so perhaps it would be better to call it "The Disciple's prayer." It is a prayer that is said by at least two billion people on a regular basis. The trouble is, this regularity can result in routine and routine can result in a lack of reality. It can cause us to forget that Jesus was encouraging us to say something radical. He was urging us to address God as "Father." What a marvel that is! This is the language of a child before his or her daddy. Jesus invites us to join a worldwide family in which everyone looks adoringly into the eyes of God and cries, "You're our Father, the Father who dwells in the heavenly realms." Now that is a revelation that ought to produce a revolution in the soul!

PRAYER

Dear Lord Jesus, I want to give You the highest praise for teaching us that God is our Heavenly Papa and for making it possible to know Him. Amen.

In The Secret Place

"This is your Father you are dealing with, and
he knows better than you what you need."
—MATTHEW 6:8

Just before Jesus teaches us to pray "Our Father in Heaven," He
tells His followers about the importance of "the secret place."
In Jesus' day, this was a word used for the storeroom where the
treasure was kept. Jesus urged us to find a quiet place and to
meet with our Father in private. He told us that our Father is
already there, waiting for us to talk with Him. He knows what
is best for us, so we can trust Him as we bring our needs before
Him. This Father is better than all the best dads in the world put
together. When we set time aside in the secret place, we encounter the Father's love. This is the greatest treasure of all. Prayer is,
accordingly, not an act of incessant and insecure imploring—it is
a trustful conversation between a child and their perfect Father.
As you read these devotions, ask the Father to come and reveal
His heart to you.

PRAYER

*Thank You, oh my Father, that prayer is not talking to
a brick wall but conversing as a child with the world's
greatest Dad. In Jesus' name. Amen.*

The Hallowed Name

"Reveal who you are."
—MATTHEW 6:9

Jesus teaches us to pray to "our Father in Heaven." He then goes on to say, "Reveal who you really are." In other translations He says, "Hallowed be your name." The word "hallow" means to hold dear, to revere, to honor and to regard as sacred. The "name" that Jesus is referring to is "Father." When we pray the simple words, "Our Father in Heaven," we make a decision to esteem highly the name "Father." Why do we do this? It is because Jesus alone reveals that God is our loving, doting, affectionate Father. If Jesus hadn't come to earth and shown us what God is really like, we would never have called God "Father." There are so many names for God in the Old and the New Testaments, but the greatest and most sacred name of all is "Father." Thank God for Jesus, who reveals who God really is.

PRAYER

Dear Lord Jesus, help me to hold the name "Father" in far greater honor as I pray to God and read these devotions, in Your precious name. Amen.

Your Kingdom Come!

"Set the world right;
Do what's best—as above, so below."
—MATTHEW 6:10

After Jesus has encouraged His followers to pray, "Our Father," He now proceeds to teach them to pray, "Your Kingdom come." What did Jesus mean by "the Kingdom of Heaven"? Heaven is the clue. In Heaven, our Father rules as King over everything. Heaven is, therefore, the place where the rule of God is so strong that sin cannot exist there, nor sickness, nor injustice, nor any other hint of the devil's work. When we pray, "Your Kingdom come," we are asking our Father to bring the reign of Heaven to those who are experiencing hell on earth. Notice how Jesus asks His followers to know and worship the Father before they usher in the Kingdom. These are the two great themes of Jesus' teaching: the Fatherhood of God and the Kingdom of God. Only those who know their Father can be used to set the world right.

PRAYER

Lord Jesus, I pray that I may know the Father more clearly, so that I may bring His rule to earth more effectively. In Your name. Amen.

Relating and Reigning

"Prosper! Reproduce! Fill Earth! Take charge!"
—GENESIS 1:28

In the beginning, Adam and Eve enjoyed two great privileges before the serpent tempted them. They first of all enjoyed the honor of relating to the Father as His children. When Adam was created, the first thing he would have been aware of was the Father's face—with love. But this was not all. To both Adam and Eve, the Father gave a mandate to bring His rule to every part of the earth outside the Garden of Eden. They were to enjoy His favor, have children, fill the earth with sons and daughters, and take charge of all that God had made. In other words, they were called to reign in life. When Adam and Eve sinned, they lost both their relationship with the Father and their authority to rule. Thank God for Jesus, who restores our lost identity as the sons and daughters of God, and who empowers us to bring the rule of Heaven to earth.

PRAYER

Help me, Jesus, to relate to the Father as a child of God and to bring the reign of Heaven to wherever I set my feet. In Your name. Amen.

Original Intimacy

...son of Adam, son of God.
—LUKE 3:38

The Gospel of Matthew and the Gospel of Luke both include a family tree of Jesus. The family tree supplied by Luke goes further back in time than Matthew's. Matthew's goes back as far as Abraham while Luke's goes back as far as Adam. There are a number of reasons for this, the most important of which is that Luke wants to emphasize that Jesus came for more than just the children of Abraham (the Jewish people). He came to rescue *everyone* from their sins. So Luke traces Jesus' lineage right back to Adam, whom he calls "son of God." That's an interesting phrase. What it shows is that our first parents experienced the closest possible communion with the Father, as His son and His daughter. That's what the devil stole; this is what Jesus takes back. Let's be a people who reflect "Paradise Regained" not "Paradise Lost." Let's walk and talk with our Father every day, as Adam and Eve did in the Garden.

PRAYER

Thank You, Jesus, for restoring our relationship with the Father. Help me to cultivate the closest communion with my Father in Heaven. Amen.

The Providing Father

"Keep us alive with three square meals."
—MATTHEW 6:11

Jesus teaches His disciples to commune with God as children before a good, good Father. One of the requests that He encourages them to pray, is for the Father's daily provision of food. Here again, how we were brought up can affect our ability to pray this with ease. If we were brought up by a father who didn't provide for us, then it may be hard for us to believe that God is a Father who provides—that God is Jehovah Jireh, Always our Provider, to use one of His most beautiful Old Testament names. We need to come to a place where we know that our Father loves us so much that He will never allow us to go without. Doesn't He provide for the birds of the air? How much more will He provide for the children He loves! Why not resolve today to forgive your earthly father if you feel that you lived in lack? As you give your earthly father your forgiveness, watch as the Holy Spirit introduces you to your true Father, whom Jesus came to reveal—a Father who gives you one blessing after another.

PRAYER

Dearest Father, I thank You that I can trust You to provide for me. I pray today and every day for You to meet my basic needs. In Jesus' name. Amen.

The Pardoning Father

"Keep us forgiven with you and forgiving others."
—MATTHEW 6:12

We looked in the previous devotion at the importance of forgiving our fathers if they failed to provide for us. This is essential if we are to come to a place of childlike trust in our Father in Heaven. If we don't forgive our earthly fathers for not loving us properly, there is every chance that we will end up believing God is like our fathers. So what does it mean to forgive? It means to give a person a gift they don't deserve. It means renouncing our desire to retaliate and have revenge. It means bringing our bitterness to the foot of the Cross and leaving it there. Forgiveness does not mean saying to someone, "What you did to me doesn't matter." It means no longer holding that against them. It means putting an end to the endless replays of past hurts in our heads. It means remembering what happened to us, but without the pain attached. When we choose to forgive others, we discover that we were never keeping the other person in prison. We were the ones in jail and we are the ones who now walk free. There is no end to the blessings of the Father's love that can be received by those who forgive others from the heart.

PRAYER

Dearest Father, help me to forgive those who have hurt me in the past, so that my heart may be an unblocked container, ready to receive Your love. Amen.

The Protecting Father

"Keep us safe from ourselves and the Devil."
—MATTHEW 6:13

Many people, when they become Christians, receive a shock. They think they are signing up for a holiday destination in the sun, only to find themselves in a war zone! Often preachers don't make it clear what the Christian life involves. Yes, our Heavenly Father provides for us and pardons us. But He also promises to protect us. We need protecting because we are in an intense spiritual conflict between the Kingdom of light and the kingdom of darkness. We are engaged in a fearsome spiritual struggle between the King of kings and the father of lies. Now the Bible is very clear about the fact that we are on the winning side and that in the end the devil will be destroyed. But until the momentous day when Jesus returns, we are fighting a battle against a malicious enemy who wants to rob us of our blessings and destroy our lives. For that reason we must come before our Heavenly Father every day and night in prayer, asking Him to keep us safe from the evil one. The good news is that we have a Father who protects us when we love and trust Him. We can nestle in His arms and feel safe.

PRAYER

Dearest Father, thank You for showing me that I'm caught up in a battle between good and evil. Please protect me and the ones I love. Amen.

Jesus, One of a Kind

This is how much God loved the world: He gave
his Son, his one and only Son. And this is why:
so that no one need be destroyed; by believing in
him, anyone can have a whole and lasting life.
—JOHN 3:16

In the previous devotion we saw how Luke referred to Adam as "Son of God." Does that mean that Jesus was not the only Son of God? Here we have to remember John 3:16. In this verse we learn about the Father's extraordinary love in giving His "one and only Son." Notice the phrase "one and only." This means "one of a kind." If Jesus is the one and only Son, then Adam must have been a different kind of son. This is indeed the case. Adam was a son who was created in time. Jesus is the Son of God from eternity to eternity. Adam was the first human being to enjoy a relationship of sonship with God. Jesus alone was able to restore what Adam lost.

PRAYER

Dear Lord Jesus, help me never to water down Your uniqueness. You truly are the one and only Son of God and I worship You with all my heart. Amen.

Father's Kingdom

"I'll not be drinking wine from this cup
again until that new day when I'll drink
with you in the kingdom of my Father."
—MATTHEW 26:29

It is so important to understand fully the relationship between the Father and the Kingdom. God gave Adam and Eve the mandate to relate to Him as His son and daughter and to bring His Kingdom to earth. That privilege was lost by the first Adam but restored by the "last Adam," Jesus. Thanks to Jesus, we can now relate to God as our loving Father and bring the Father's Kingdom to every place where we have influence. The Kingdom of God is therefore the powerful presence of the Father's love. Wherever the royally adopted sons and daughters of God choose to serve, there they bring the Father's love. In that realm, sins are forgiven, injustices are addressed, sicknesses are healed, and the devil's hold over lives is broken. Nothing can stand against the powerful presence of the Father's love. Let's bring the Father's Kingdom to earth.

PRAYER

*Dear Father, help me every day to bring the powerful
presence of Your love to my family, my workplace, my
spheres of influence. In Jesus' name. Amen.*

Without Partiality

"You're kingdom subjects. Now live like it.
Live out your God-created identity. Live
generously and graciously toward others,
the way God lives toward you."
—MATTHEW 5:48

In the NIV translation this verse says, "Be perfect, therefore, as your Heavenly Father is perfect." What did Jesus mean by "perfect"? If you read the rest of the passage you'll see that He's been teaching about not just loving the people you like but loving your enemies as well. There's no reward in loving the people that are kind to you. But there's a great reward in loving the people who hate you and make your life difficult. This is what Jesus means by perfect. Being perfect means living generously and graciously toward those who oppose you. It means loving without partiality. Why is this so important? It is because this is what the Father does. He loves those who are not His friends. When we love in this way, we show that we are sons and daughters of our Father. We reveal our true identity as His children. Let's resolve to embrace the Father's perfection and love without partiality. This is the Kingdom of Heaven!

PRAYER

*Dear Father, I thank You that You love perfectly,
without partiality. Teach me to reveal this perfect love
in my relationships too. In Jesus' name. Amen.*

A Sign of Sonship

*"You're blessed when you can show people
how to cooperate instead of compete or fight.
That's when you discover who you really
are, and your place in God's family."*
—MATTHEW 5:9

In recent devotions we have been looking at our two greatest tasks—to be in such intimate communion with the Father that we bring the powerful presence of His love to those around us. One of the hallmarks of those who fulfill this commission is that they bring the Father's peace into situations of conflict. As another translation of the verse above puts it, "Blessed are the peacemakers, for they shall be called the sons of God." If we want to be known as Abba's children, then we need to show people how they can cooperate instead of compete or fight. This is when we discover who we really are—the sons and daughters of God! This is when the world discovers who we really are. God is our Peace and Christ is our Peacemaker. When we engage in the ministry of reconciliation, we bring the Kingdom of Heaven to earth.

PRAYER

*Dear Father, help me to reveal my true identity as
Your son, Your daughter, by bringing peace and
reconciliation into my world. In Jesus' name. Amen.*

Shining for My Father

"Keep open house; be generous with your lives. By opening up to others, you'll prompt people to open up with God, this generous Father in heaven."
—MATTHEW 5:16

Another translation of this verse goes as follows: "In the same way, let your light shine before others, that they may see your good deeds and glorify your Father in Heaven." One of the simplest ways in which we can bring the Father's Kingdom to earth is by being kind to other people. When we open our homes to those who are lonely and unloved, when we behave as good neighbors, when we help those in need, when we show compassion to the homeless, then we become brilliant sons and daughters of our Father in Heaven. Jesus makes it very clear: when we perform acts of kindness, we become shiny with the Father's love and we cause those who don't know God to turn in wonder toward the One who lives within us. Let's resolve to become radiant sons and daughters. Let's show kindness in our community.

PRAYER

Abba, Father, I ask You to help me to show Your love to those around me and to become more luminous for You, that Your name might be glorified. Amen.

A Kindness Revolution

"Our Father is kind; you be kind."
—LUKE 6:36

Kindness is one of the most beautiful qualities. When a person is kind to another, especially when others are unable to help themselves, it creates a ripple effect in which people want to show love toward others. Kindness is contagious. In an unkind world, Jesus wants His followers to be the kindest people on the earth. The Father's Kingdom is a Kingdom of kindness. Jesus is the King of kindness. He was kind to those whom the world marginalized and ostracized—sinners, prostitutes, lepers, and tax collectors. When we show this kind of kindness to those who hate us, or who are hated by those around us, it is radical. The Father's love is a subversive love; it is counterintuitive and countercultural. Let's start a revolution of kindness in our families, communities, workplaces and world. There are few things as powerful as the Father's kindness.

PRAYER

Dear Father, I thank You that You excel in the virtue of kindness. Help me to excel in this quality too. Help me to start a kindness revolution. Amen.

Serious Obedience

"Knowing the correct password—saying 'Master,
Master,' for instance—isn't going to get you
anywhere with me. What is required is serious
obedience—doing what my Father wills."
—MATTHEW 7:21

Jesus makes it plain that saying the right things is not enough to
get us anywhere with Him. We need to do the right things too.
This means that there are two very important foundations for
our relationship with the Father. The first is intimacy—knowing
Him deeply, relationally, and personally. We do this only through
Jesus and in the power of the Holy Spirit. There is no other way.
The second is purity. We must live holy lives, doing everything
Jesus commands—a lifestyle that He calls "serious obedience."
So it is not enough to talk about intimacy with the Father. If we
want to be authentic sons and daughters of God, then we must
make it our aim always to do what our Father wants, not what we
want. This may mean we have to pay a price, but the true sons and
daughters of God are prepared to suffer with Jesus. They are prepared to lay down their lives daily, putting self last and Jesus first.
So let's resolve not just to talk the talk, but let's walk the walk too!

PRAYER

*Dearest Father, help me to be an obedient child of God
and to cultivate a lifestyle of serious obedience as I
follow Your Son. In His name. Amen.*

My Father's Spirit

"Don't worry about what you'll say or how
you'll say it. The right words will be there; the
Spirit of your Father will supply the words."
—MATTHEW 10:19–20

Sometimes we experience intense opposition because of our faith in Jesus. This is not a rational hostility at all. Oftentimes it occurs within cultures that value tolerance—tolerance for everyone, that is, except those who truly believe in Jesus! How are we to react when others criticize and condemn us for our Christian faith? Jesus tells us. We are not to worry about how to answer them. We are to rest in our position as the adopted sons and daughters of God and allow the Spirit of our Father to supply the words. If you are in a situation where you are being persecuted for your faith, pray for the Spirit of your Father to work through you so that you can bring Heaven's words into the situation, not your own. The Father's words carry wisdom from another world!

PRAYER

*Dear Lord Jesus, I pray in Your mighty name for more
of the Spirit of my Father whenever I am put on the spot
for my faith in You. Amen.*

A Childlike Love

"I'm telling you, once and for all, that unless
you return to square one and start over
like children, you're not even going to get a
look at the kingdom, let alone get in."
—MATTHEW 18:3

How does a person enter the Father's Kingdom? The answer is by becoming a child all over again. In a sense, this is what Jesus said to Nicodemus when He said, "You must be born again" (see John 3:3). A person who wants to see the powerful presence of the Father's love must first of all position themselves as a child before the Father. There is really no other way. Jesus doesn't tell children to embrace the sophistication of adults. He tells adults to embrace the simplicity of children. Unless we humble ourselves and become childlike, we will never see the reign of Heaven come to earth. We have to recognize that entering this Kingdom and seeing this Kingdom are both dependent on us being like little children before our perfect Heavenly Father. The revelation of the Father's love comes to the simple, not the sophisticated.

PRAYER

Help me, Lord Jesus, to embrace the simple faith of a child. Thank You that it is the childlike ones who see Heaven on earth. In Your name. Amen.

No More Walls

> The Samaritan woman, taken aback, asked,
> "How come you, a Jew, are asking me, a Samaritan
> woman, for a drink?" (Jews in those days wouldn't
> be caught dead talking to Samaritans.)
> —JOHN 4:9

Early on in Jesus' ministry He reveals the Father's heart in the most extraordinary way. It all begins with Jesus sitting down at a well in Samaria. A Samaritan woman comes to the well at noon, hoping to be there alone. Jesus, however, is sitting there on His own, tired and thirsty, and asks her for a drink. This is radical behavior. Jews did not associate with Samaritans. Jewish men thought Samaritan women were the lowest of the low. As a rabbi, Jesus should have taken 20 steps back. But He doesn't, because He wants to give the Father's love to one of the untouchables. Do you see the Father's heart here? The true children of the Father do not build walls, they build bridges. Our song should always be, "We will break dividing walls." This is the Father's heart.

PRAYER

*Dear Lord Jesus, I thank You that the Father loves **everybody.** Help me to bring this awesome love to those whom others despise. In Your name. Amen.*

Living Water

> "If you knew the generosity of God and who
> I am, you would be asking me for a drink,
> and I would give you fresh, living water."
> —JOHN 4: 10

We continue with the story of Jesus and the Samaritan woman. Jesus asks her for a drink as He sits at a well in Samaria. She tells Him that He shouldn't be associating with her because of the racial and gender divide between them. Jesus ignores that and tells her that He wants to give her "fresh, living water." Here Jesus addresses the woman's true need—not for the still water of the well but the river of life. This is the Father's heart—to fill the spiritual void in people's lives with His great and generous love. Jesus knows that this woman's true desire is for love and so He takes time to appeal to the hole in her soul by talking about "living water." By this He means the Holy Spirit, which will be poured out at Pentecost. The Holy Spirit, also called "the Spirit of adoption" in the New Testament, will fill her aching heart and meet her deepest need. What a good, good Father we have!

PRAYER

Father, I bring to You my deepest thirst, and ask You to quench it with the living, fresh and sparkling waters of Your love. In Jesus' name. Amen.

Gushing Fountains

"The water I give will be an artesian spring
within, gushing fountains of endless life."
—JOHN 4:14

There are two Greek words translated "life." There is first of all *bios,* from which we get the word "biology." This refers to finite, creaturely existence. Then there is the word *zoe,* which means "infinite, abundant life." Jesus is talking here with the Samaritan woman at the well. She is simply surviving on a day-to-day basis, but Jesus wants more for her than that. He has come that she might have *zoe* life. This is the Father's heart for her and indeed for all of us, that by believing in Jesus and receiving the Holy Spirit we should find salvation and satisfaction. More than that, as we receive this life-giving water, the Father's longing is that we will become gushing fountains of endless life, giving the Father's love and life to others. Let's not keep the Love of all loves to ourselves. Let's be conduits of this love to others.

PRAYER

Father, help me not to be a lake but a river. Help me not to keep Your life-giving love to myself, but give it away generously to others. In Jesus' name. Amen.

The Seventh Man

"You've had five husbands, and the man you're
living with now isn't even your husband. You
spoke the truth there, sure enough."
—JOHN 4:18

When Jesus offers the Samaritan the gift of living water, she
becomes excited and asks for some. Jesus tells her to go back and
bring her husband, so that he can share in the joy. She says that
she doesn't have a husband. Jesus replies that she has had five and
that the man she's living with now is not her husband. Notice
how the number of men this woman has been with is six. What
does that make Jesus? It makes Him the seventh man. Why is
that important? Seven is a significant number in Judaism—it
symbolizes perfection. All the previous men in this woman's life
have been imperfect. Jesus is the perfect man, and Him alone.
What a wonderful truth this is! This woman has been looking
for love in very imperfect places. Now she has found it in Jesus,
who offers her the Father's love—the perfect love that alone satisfies the aching heart.

PRAYER

*Jesus, I worship You that You are truly the perfect man,
because You alone reveal the Father's love and release
that love into our empty souls. Amen.*

A Great Embrace

"The time is coming when you Samaritans
will worship the Father."
—JOHN 4:21

It is so interesting to see how the conversation with the Samaritan woman progresses. Jesus has just seen right into her heart and revealed her deepest secrets. The woman is astonished. At this point, you might expect Jesus to talk about her need for forgiveness but He doesn't. He talks to her about *worship*. In the original language, the word for worship—which Jesus uses seven times in this conversation—means "to approach someone in order to kiss them." What Jesus is inviting this woman into is the Father's embrace. He is saying to her that in the future she and her people will be able to find salvation and satisfaction in approaching the Father and embracing Him in worship. This is what worship is. It is drawing near to the Father in order to say, "I love you." This is the Father's heart for us.

PRAYER

*Father, help me to understand that the heart of worship
is choosing to draw near to You to embrace You, to tell
You that I love You. In Jesus' name. Amen.*

Jesus Is for Everyone!

"God's way of salvation is made
available through the Jews."
—JOHN 4:22

Here again we see the Father's heart. Jesus is talking to a Samaritan woman. There are two things going against her. The first is that she is a Samaritan. The Samaritans were despised by the Jews because they were a hybrid nation—a mixture of Jews and other nations. The second is that she is a woman. In public, Jewish men steered clear of women they didn't know. Jesus rejects all that and offers this woman the gift of the Father's love. He states that "salvation is from the Jews." The word He uses for salvation would have been *yeshua* in the Aramaic language that He spoke. *Yeshua* is Jesus' name! Jesus—that is to say "salvation"—comes from the Jewish people because Jesus is a Jew. But Jesus also makes it abundantly clear that although salvation is from the Jews, it is available to every nation under the sun, including the hated Samaritans. See how great the Father's love is for humankind. He loves everyone, especially victims of racial and sexual prejudice.

PRAYER

*Dear Lord Jesus, help me to be more like You. Help
me to show and share the Father's saving love to those
whom my society rejects. In Your name. Amen.*

Heaven's Longing

"Your worship must engage your spirit in
the pursuit of truth. That's the kind of
people the Father is out looking for."
—JOHN 4:23

Our loving Heavenly Father is looking for people all over the world who will worship Him in spirit and in truth. This is what Jesus says to the Samaritan woman at the well. What does Jesus mean here? Keep in mind that worship is drawing near to the Father to tell Him that we adore Him, even as He adores us. To do this we need two things. We need Jesus who is the Truth. This is what is meant by "in truth." We also need the Holy Spirit, because it is by this Spirit that our love for the Father becomes an experiential reality in our lives. This is what is meant by "in spirit." If we want to approach our Father every day and feel His embrace, then we must come to Him through Jesus, and we must do so in the Holy Spirit, who pours out the Father's love in our hearts. This is what Father is looking for.

PRAYER

*Thank You, my Father, for giving us both Your Son
and Your Spirit, so that I might know You personally
and love You deeply. In Jesus' name. Amen.*

Crazy About God

*"Those who worship him must do it out of their very
being, their spirits, their true selves, in adoration."*
—JOHN 4:24

Jesus is finishing His explanation about worship to the Samaritan woman at the well. As He ends this teaching—the most in-depth teaching on true worship in the entire New Testament—He tells her that everyone who worships the Father must adore Him from the deepest parts of themselves. Jesus here uses the word "spirit" to describe this part of our being. The spirit is the part of us that was created by God to commune with Him in intimate love. When a person comes to Jesus, this spirit—which was formerly dead in sin—is now made alive in love. When that happens, we instinctively want to give God the highest praise. We want to tell Him that we are crazy about Him, even as He is crazy about us. True worship means loving our Heavenly Father with all we have—emotionally, intellectually, physically and spiritually. Our Father is the best, so He deserves the best.

PRAYER

*Dear God, You are the best Father in the universe, and
I absolutely adore You with all my heart, mind, body
and soul. In Jesus' name. Amen.*

Holy Desperation

> The woman said, "I don't know about that. I do
> know that the Messiah is coming. When he arrives,
> we'll get the whole story." "I am he," said Jesus.
> —JOHN 4:25–26

The Samaritan woman has been listening to Jesus talking about her worshipping the Father. As He finishes, she tells Him that her people are longing for the Messiah. When He comes, then they will know the whole story about true worship. Jesus replies with a very simple statement. In the original Greek, He says, "I, I Am." This is a history-making moment, not only for the woman but for all of us. "I Am" was the ancient, Hebrew name for God. When God revealed His name to Moses, He told Him, "I Am who I Am." What Jesus is doing here is revealing who He truly is—Jehovah God in human flesh! This is the first time in His ministry that He reveals His divinity—and it is to a Samaritan woman! This is so in keeping with the Father's love. He doesn't reveal Himself to the satisfied, but to the thirsty. The Father's love is truly for the desperate.

PRAYER

*I worship You Jesus, that You are the Great I Am who
has shown the Father's love to the desperate. I am thirsty
for more of that love. In Your name. Amen.*

Dropping Everything

The woman took the hint and left. In her
confusion she left her water pot.
—John 4:28

This is a priceless moment in the story about Jesus' encounter with the Samaritan woman at the well. The story starts with Jesus asking the woman for a drink. When Jesus finishes talking with her, she drops her water jar and rushes back into town. So Jesus never did get that drink. But the woman did. She got to taste the Father's love. This was what she had been waiting for all her life. Up until this point she had been looking for love in all the wrong places. She was what today we would call a relationship addict. But now she has found true love, not in other men, but in the Father's love—the love that Jesus came to reveal, to the outcasts and the sinners. What an amazing Savior we have in Jesus! He knows our deepest needs. It is the Father's love alone that causes us to drop our pots with unbridled joy.

PRAYER

Dear Jesus, I thank You for introducing me to the Father I've been waiting for all my life. I want to drop everything to know His love. In Your name. Amen.

Conduits of Love

She told the people, "Come see a man who knew all
about the things I did, who knows me inside and out."
—JOHN 4:29

At the beginning of her encounter with Jesus, the Samaritan woman was invited at a physical well to become a spiritual well—one that poured out the Father's love to everyone. This is precisely what she becomes. When she meets Jesus, she tastes the Father's love and finds it so deeply satisfying that she can't hold herself back; she rushes into town to tell everyone about the One who knows her inside and out. What a wonderful example she is. Without any encouragement, without any training, she immediately becomes an ambassador of the Father's love to everyone in her community. Having received an invitation to love, she now issues invitations to everyone in her town of Sychar. What would happen if we allowed ourselves to be captivated by the Father's love in this way? There would be revival everywhere!

PRAYER

*Dear Jesus, help me to become an ambassador of the
Father's love, and to invite everyone I know to taste and
see that the Father is good. In Your name. Amen.*

Banquets for the Broken

"He takes in sinners and eats meals with
them, treating them like old friends."
—LUKE 15:2

Jesus stirred up controversy in his own day, especially among groups such as the teachers of the law. The main problem He had with them was that they were turning a law of love into a love of law. They taught that only those who obeyed the law in every detail stood a chance of getting close to God. Jesus completely turned this on its head and He did this through His actions, first and foremost. Here, in this verse, we see what He did. He had meals with messed-up people. This open meal table sent a very clear message to the teachers of the law. "Stop misrepresenting God. God is not an angry lawyer who excludes people. He is a loving Father who embraces everyone, especially those who are really, really broken, and who know and admit they are broken." What a beautiful picture these meals provide. They are actions that reveal the open arms of the Father.

PRAYER

*Dear Father, teach me to have my arms open wide to
those who are broken, and to reflect Your heart in an
attitude of embrace, not exclusion. Amen.*

A Powerful Trilogy

Their grumbling triggered this story.
—LUKE 15:2

In the previous devotion we saw how the teachers of the law put walls around the presence of God. If you obeyed the law in every tiny detail, then you could climb over these walls through your own self-effort and draw near to Him. If not, you were excluded. Jesus responds by holding meals in which the people who were most excluded by these teachers were most welcome. More than that, He reacts by telling three powerful stories—about a lost sheep, a lost coin and a lost son. This trilogy showcases one important theme—the Father pursues the lost, the last and the least, just as the shepherd seeks the lost sheep, the woman looks for the lost coin, and the father runs after the lost boy. What a great way of challenging those with an exclusive impulse. Jesus holds meals and tells gripping stories, all of which communicate the Father's pursuant and inclusive love. These all pose a question to the legalistic leaders of His day: "Do you have eyes to see, ears to hear and a heart to understand the Father heart of God?"

PRAYER

Dearest Father, thank You for Your compassion
for the lost, the last and the least. Please help me to
demonstrate this love today. In Jesus' name. Amen.

Misrepresenting God

"Count on it—that's the kind of party God's angels
throw every time one lost soul turns to God."
—LUKE 15:10

Jesus is responding to the teachers of the law who have been complaining to Him that He holds parties with prostitutes. They don't like the fact that the people they regarded as the most unclean of all are finding a great and heartfelt welcome at Jesus' meal tables. This makes them mad! Jesus responds by telling three parables— the lost sheep, the lost coin and the lost boy. Parables are basically small stories with big ideas. They are down-to-earth tales that highlight heavenly principles. What's the point that Jesus is making in the three parables that He tells here? It's quite simple if you have eyes to see. Each of these stories ends with a great celebration. When the shepherd, the woman and the father find what is lost, they have a party to which everyone around is invited. What could be clearer than that? Jesus uses these stories to bring a stinging rebuke to His listeners: "Stop misrepresenting God. God is not an aloof lawyer. He's an affectionate Father." More than that, Jesus says directly, "My Father throws a party with all the angels when a lost soul turns to Him." This truly is the Father's heart.

PRAYER

*Dear Jesus, help me never to misrepresent God. Teach
me more and more of the Father's heart so that the
broken ones may always feel welcome. Amen.*

The Greatest Dad

"There was once a man who had two sons."
—LUKE 15:11

Jesus tells three stories in order to refute the legalism of His listeners. He tells about a lost sheep, a lost coin and a lost boy. These parables reveal that God is the most extravagantly loving and compassionate Father in the universe—a Father who believes in embrace not exclusion; who adores the lost, the last and the least; who is so crazy about imperfect people that He will go to any lengths to woo them into His arms of love. Perhaps nowhere in the Bible is this truth more clearly illustrated than in the parable of the prodigal son. Here Jesus tells a story about "a man who had two sons." This sentence reveals the hero of the tale—not the boy who becomes lost, but the father who never stops loving him, or his older brother for that matter. In the coming devotions we are going to learn how everything we see in this extraordinary father is a window onto our Father's heart. We will see that this dad goes far further than any Middle Eastern dad of his day would have gone. In the process, we will see how this is a picture in miniature of the greatest dad ever—our Father in Heaven.

PRAYER

Thank You, Jesus for telling this timeless story of an astonishing dad. Give me eyes to see my Heavenly Father in every detail. In Your name. Amen.

A Patient Love

> "The younger said to his father, 'Father, I
> want right now what's coming to me.'"
> —LUKE 15:12

The first thing we learn about this dad is that he is extremely patient. When his younger son comes to him, he makes a scandalous request. He asks for his inheritance right now. Why is that scandalous? In the Middle Eastern culture of Jesus' day, no son ever asked for his inheritance while his dad was still alive. That was a shameful thing to do. It was effectively saying, "I wish you were dead now." The astonishing thing about this father is that he agrees! Even though his son is dishonoring him, even though his son is effectively rejecting him, the father says "yes." Now keep in mind what we've been learning in these devotions. *The father in the story is a picture in miniature of our Father in Heaven.* That being the case, we can see the extreme patience of God. Our Father is constantly being rejected by people. But in all of this, He never stops loving us. His love never gives up. It never fails. It never diminishes. What an extraordinarily patient Father! Aren't you grateful that He is patient with you?

PRAYER

*Thank You, dear Father, that You are so patient with
me, that You never stop loving me, even when I falter,
fail and fall. In Jesus' name. Amen.*

A Radical Love

"So the father divided the property between them."
—LUKE 15:12

The younger son in the story has rejected his dad. Many parents will know how that feels. When a son or a daughter rebels against a parent's love, the pain is beyond description. How will the dad in the story respond? He reacts by giving the boy what he's requested. Most parents would have said "no" and punished their child. This father does something extremely radical. What is that? *He gives the boy what he wants so that the boy can discover in due time what he really needs—his father's love.* Isn't that like our Heavenly Father? How often has God allowed us to have what we want in our flesh so that we can learn, through the emptiness that always follows, what we really need in our spirit? We are so like rebellious children. We think we know what's best for us and God allows us sometimes to have it, so that we come to see in the end that only our Father in Heaven knows what really satisfies—His radical love.

PRAYER

Father, help me to focus on what I really need, not on what I think I want. Help me to focus on experiencing Your love first. In Jesus' name. Amen.

A Watching Love

"When he was still a long way off, his father saw him."
—LUKE 15:20

The inevitable happens. The younger son in the story takes his dad's hard-earned money and squanders it all. He ends up being so broke that he has to take on a job in a pigpen—not a good place for a Jewish boy. He then comes to his senses and thinks, "I'll go back to my dad." How many days later do you think this was? It could have been months, years even. What was his father doing in the meantime? He was watching out for his returning son, yearning in his heart for his boy, sighing and crying for a reunion. Then one day he saw a silhouette in the distance—the outline of a bedraggled man, limping across the desert sand—and he is overjoyed. What a great picture this is of our Father. He never gives up. He keeps watching and waiting, longing for us to come home. This boy lost everything, except one thing—his father's love. We too can lose everything, but there's one thing we can never lose—our Father's love.

PRAYER

Thank You, dear Father that You never stop watching out for the return of Your prodigals. Bring them all home soon. In Jesus' name. Amen.

A Compassionate Love

"His heart pounding."
—LUKE 15:20

The father has been watching for many months, years even, for his lost boy to return. Then one day, he sees him. How does he feel? The Bible says that his heart was pounding. In the original language, we read that he felt a sharp pain, as if his intestines were being ripped apart. What does that mean? It means this father was moved in the most visceral part of his being. What emotion did he feel? Was it rage? Was it relief? The answer is that it was compassion. This father felt a gut-wrenching sense of pity for his boy—not a condescending pity, but a heartfelt pity, one in which the father experienced such a degree of empathy that he found himself suffering with his destitute and desperate son. This, again, is a picture of our Father in Heaven. He is not aloof, as the ancient Greeks understood Him. No, in Jesus, He is Immanuel. He is God with us. He feels what we feel. He is a sympathetic not an apathetic Father. Thank God that He is slow to anger and rich in unfailing, compassionate love.

PRAYER

Dearest Father, I give You praise for the fact that You feel what we feel and that Your heart breaks with compassionate love for Your children. Amen.

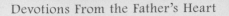

A Pursuant Love

"He ran out."
—LUKE 15:20

When the father sees his boy, he feels deep compassion. What does he do? The Bible says he ran out to his returning son. There are a number of revealing things about this. First, it is counter-cultural. It was the repentant son's place to run to his father, not the other way round. Second, it is merciful. The father runs to his boy because he wants to get to him before the villagers. If they get there first, they will insult him for bringing such shame upon his father's house. Third, it is beautiful. The verb that is used here for running really means racing. This father ran like the wind to get to his boy. That's truly beautiful. Finally, it is radical. This father was probably well over thirty years of age. In those days, no man over thirty ran in public, because it would mean pulling up their robe and revealing their undergarments. This father is so over-whelmed by love he just doesn't care. See what a great picture this is of the Father's heart. His love is a pursuant love—He pursues us with everything He has, so that our shame can be replaced by His honor. What a good, good Father we have.

PRAYER

Dearest Father, I want to worship You and give You praise that even while I was far away from You, You came looking for me. In Jesus' name. Amen.

A Hugging Love

"He embraced him."
—LUKE 15:20

If you imagine it for a moment, the younger son has been sleeping with the pigs in the far country. He must have been disheveled, destitute and covered in dirt—so much so the father probably smelt the boy before he saw him! In other words, the boy was thoroughly unclean. But this dad doesn't care. All he cares about is getting to his boy before the villagers, because the villagers want to exclude the son, while the father wants to embrace him. And that is exactly what he does. He falls upon his son's shoulders and holds him tight. What a great picture this is of our good, good Father in Heaven. When we return to Him, when we come home with true sorrow over our sins, He doesn't stand at a distance, nor is He aloof. No, He embraces us in spite of our sinfulness. He holds us in spite of the dirt in our lives. How great is our God! He truly hugs the hell out of us!

PRAYER

Dearest Father, please hug the hell out of me today.
In Your embrace, let all my sin and sorrow flee away.
Make me new in Your arms, I pray. Amen.

A Demonstrative Love

"He kissed him."
—LUKE 15:20

Picture the scene. The son has rejected his dad, and rebelled against his love. Squandering his father's fortune, he has lost everything and ended up in disgrace. Now he has returned, and finds that his father, far from rejecting him, has run to him with weeping eyes and thrown his arms around him. What happens next? The Bible says that the father "kissed Him". The verb is actually in the continuous tense so it means that the dad kissed him *repeatedly*. The verb is also in the intensive, so it means that the dad kissed him *earnestly* as well! That was not what this son expected. It's not what many children today expect from their fathers either. Many dads don't know how to express their love in open and tender ways. Maybe their own fathers didn't show affection, and they are simply passing this detachment to the next generation. How different is the father in this story. His love is unashamedly demonstrative. And so is our Father's. He doesn't stand at a distance. He embraces us and kisses us. When we return to Him, we feel His love. We experience the kiss of Heaven.

PRAYER

*Dearest Father, help me to encounter Your love today.
I ask for the kiss of Heaven, and for the experience of
being enfolded in Your arms. Amen.*

A Gracious Love

"The father wasn't listening."
—LUKE 15:22

The younger son has returned and is now being kissed over and over again by his weeping father. The son tries to respond by starting the speech he has rehearsed time and again in his heart. "Father, I'm sorry. Please take me on as a hired servant on your estate. Maybe I can pay you back through hard work." We should note two things here. Firstly, the son only gives half of his pre-pared speech. He never says the part about being a servant. Secondly, the father isn't listening anyway. You see the father doesn't want his boy to be a servant. He wants to restore him as a son. This is important. Jesus is using the father in this story to paint a picture of our Father in Heaven. God doesn't want ser-vants, who seek to earn His love through performance. He wants sons and daughters, who rest in His love because of their posi-tion. This is momentous. Law says, "You have to merit God's love." Grace says, "You simply have to receive God's love." Aren't you grateful that the Father's love is a gracious love?

PRAYER

Dearest Father, I want to celebrate Your amazing grace, the love that gives me what I don't deserve—the status of being Your daughter, Your son. Amen.

A Forgiving Love

"Bring a clean set of clothes and dress him."
—LUKE 15:22

In the original language, the father turns to his servants and orders them to fetch a robe. What robe was this? It was a special garment kept in a safe place in the father's house and reserved for visiting dignitaries. Why does he do this? It is because he wants to perform an action that speaks louder than words—an action that will cause everyone to marvel at his love. By covering the boy with this robe, the father sends out a very clear signal: "I forgive my son instantly, unconditionally, completely—no strings attached." What a picture this is of our Father in Heaven. Isn't this exactly what the Father has done for us through His Son, Jesus Christ? When we return to the Father in repentance, He instantly, unconditionally and completely forgives us—no strings attached. He throws the robe of Christ's righteousness over our unrighteousness and gives us a gift we don't deserve—His total forgiveness. No wonder the son is unable to finish his prepared talk. He is speechless, and so should we be too.

PRAYER

Dearest Father, I am speechless with amazement that
You offer me every day the gift of total forgiveness
because of what Jesus has done on the Cross. Amen.

A Restorative Love

"Put the family ring on his finger."
—LUKE 15:22

When he came of age, every son in Jesus' day wore a family signet ring on the fourth finger of his right hand. This ring did two things. First, it reminded everyone of this boy's identity as the father's son. Second, it signaled this boy's authority—that he had the right to give orders in the father's name. When the prodigal rebelled against his father's love, he lost the right to wear this ring. But when he came home, the father not only told the servants to bring the robe. He ordered them to bring the family signet ring and put it on the boy's finger. Notice the difference between the two gifts. If the robe gives the boy a sense of pardon, the ring gives him a sense of position. Now his identity and authority are restored. Here again, we see how this father reflects our Father's heart. When we come to Jesus, our Father not only pardons us, but He also gives us the identity and authority of sons and daughters.

PRAYER

Dearest Father, I put the ring on my finger and I revel in the fact that I'm Your child, able to use Your authority on earth. In Jesus' name. Amen.

A Liberating Love

"And sandals on his feet."
—LUKE 15:22

When the prodigal son comes home, he receives three gifts. The first is the robe, the second the ring, and the third a new pair of sandals. Actually, the original manuscripts read "leather shoes." Leather shoes are very different from sandals: sandals were the footwear of slaves; leather shoes were the footwear of the free. Do you see the importance of the father's three gifts? The first says, "You're forgiven." The second says, "You're family." The third says, "You're free!" This is what our Heavenly Father wants for us. When we come home into His arms of love, He wants us to know total forgiveness through the work of the Cross. This is the gift of justification. He wants us to know that we are the children of God through the work of His Spirit. This is the gift of adoption. Finally, He wants us to become free from all that would make us slaves again, especially sin. This is the gift of sanctification. Are you truly enjoying freedom in Christ? Have you put on Your shoes today?

PRAYER

Dear Lord Jesus, I want to receive everything that You paid for when You died for my sins on the Cross, including freedom from sin. In Your name. Amen.

A Generous Love

"Then get a grain-fed heifer and roast it."
—LUKE 15:23

The prodigal son has now returned and he is standing before his father. He hears his dad tell the servants to get a robe, a ring, and a new pair of shoes. That would have been enough. But now he hears him tell the servants to roast a fatted calf. Most people in Jesus' day may not have eaten prime roast beef like this before. More than that, there would have been enough for about two hundred people—that's the entire village, not just the father's household. It's hard not to be moved by the father's generosity here. In fact, it's interesting to note that the word "prodigal" means "extravagant." Who is the true prodigal in the story? Is it the son? Or is it the father? If the son is extravagant in his wastefulness, the father is extravagant in his lavishness. Once again, Jesus provides a glimpse of our Father in Heaven. He has lavished His love upon us with extreme generosity. He has given us the incomparable and unsearchable riches of His amazing grace. What a good, good Father He is!

PRAYER

Thank You, Dearest Father that You are not a mean and stingy father, but the most lavish Father in the universe. In Jesus' name. Amen.

A Rejoicing Love

"We're going to feast! We're going
to have a wonderful time!"
—LUKE 15:23

Jesus told the parables of the lost sheep, the lost coin, and the lost boy to make a point to the teachers of the law who were moaning that Jesus was holding meals for messed-up and sinful people. Jesus replies by telling stories which end in parties. The point He's making is a simple one: God's not a miserable killjoy legalist who wants to exclude lost people. Rather, He's the most wonderful Father who loves holding parties for people who come home to His arms in repentance. It's no surprise, then, to find that this is exactly what the dad does in the third of the three parables. When his son comes home, this father decides to hold a stupendous party, with a barbeque to beat all barbeques at the very heart of it. How utterly countercultural that must have been for Jesus' listeners. The last thing they would have said about God is that He's a joyful Father who throws parties for lost people. But that's exactly who He is, and Jesus uses this story to herald the fact that God is into the law of love, not the love of law. Let's be sure to represent God in the way that Jesus did.

PRAYER

Dearest Father, please touch my heart so deeply with the revelation of Your affection that I pursue the law of love not the love of law. Amen.

A Scandalous Love

"The older brother stalked off in an
angry sulk and refused to join in."
—LUKE 15:28

When the younger son comes home, the elder son is horrified. He cannot believe that his father would hold a party for him, so he stalks off in a rage. What is going on here? Why does Jesus not end the story with the younger son home and the party in full swing? It's because He's speaking to the teachers of the law who were outraged that He was having meals with sinners. They believed that if Jesus was truly the Messiah He would not be doing this. Now here's the point. What were the teachers of the law known as? The Elders. What is the second brother called? The "elder" son—exactly the same word. Jesus wants His listeners to know that they are reacting to the extravagant love of the Father just as the elder son does in the story. They regard such love as scandalous, and that is exactly what it is. Let's make sure that we never react to the Father's inclusive love in the way the elder son does.

PRAYER

*Dearest Father, please erase every hint of the elder son
in my heart, and help me to celebrate, not denigrate or
just tolerate Your scandalous love. Amen.*

A Relentless Love

"His father came out and tried to talk
to him, but he wouldn't listen."
—LUKE 15:28

Think about it for a moment. Earlier on this same day, the father in this story ran out to meet his returning, younger son. That was not what protocol demanded. Custom demanded that the son ran to the father. Now, later on, the elder son refuses to join in the celebrations. Where is the father? He is in the party. How does he react? He comes out to his angry son. This, again, is not what protocol demanded. The elder brother should have gone in to the party. See how relentless is this father's love? Twice on the same day he acts in a countercultural way. This should be a warning to all of us. God's love is far bigger than many of our beliefs and customs. It is a love that confounds our expectations and subverts our speculations. Our Father's love is higher, wider, stronger, and longer than we could ever dream or imagine. Let's not be offended by it. Let's be exhilarated by it.

PRAYER

*Dearest Father, I thank You that You never stop
exceeding all our expectations with Your relentless and
pursuant love. In Jesus' name. Amen.*

A Filial Love

"Look how many years I've stayed here serving you."
—LUKE 15:29

John Wesley distinguished three types of people: the *carnal* person, who does whatever his sinful nature dictates; the *legal* person, who slaves away observing religious rituals and obeying religious regulations in the hope that he can earn God's acceptance; the *filial* person who knows that he is a son and that he is forgiven, accepted, adopted and loved by the Father. Which of these three is the elder son in the parable? The answer is, he is the *legal* person. He has been slaving away for years to earn the kind of party that is now being held for a boy who doesn't deserve it at all. The point is this: our Father doesn't want us to be like the younger son (the *carnal* man), or the elder son (the *legal* man). He wants us to be like the third son—the one telling the story (the *filial* man). The Father wants us to move beyond the *carnal* and the *legal* to the *filial* state. He wants us to be like Jesus, enjoying the assurance that we are the much-loved daughters and sons of God.

PRAYER

Dearest Father, help me not to be like the younger son or the elder son, but like Your own Son, and to know forever that I am loved. In Jesus' name. Amen.

A Constant Love

"You're with me all the time, and
everything that is mine is yours."
—LUKE 15:31

It can be hard when a person who has been serving God all their life sees someone completely outside the Church have an experience of the Father's love. Perhaps the person is a drug addict who experiences a dramatic conversion, and then shares a testimony of being set free completely from their addiction in a powerful encounter with God. To someone who has been serving God all their life, and who has never experienced God's love in such an intensive way, it can be hard not to be resentful. If we find ourselves beginning to sulk, then we have forgotten what the father in the story says to the elder son—"everything I have has been available to you every day." In other words, the Father's love has been constantly available. All we have to do is stop looking at God as a Master to be served, and start seeing Him as a Father to be loved. When we do this, we move from slavery to sonship and we begin to have a continuous sense of His affection. Let's remember, the Father's love is a constant love. All we have to do is receive it each and every day!

PRAYER

*Dearest Father, Your love is like a never-ending stream.
Help me to drink from it every day and celebrate when
others are drenched in it too! Amen.*

Sustained by Sonship

"This is my Son, marked by my love. Listen to him."
—MARK 9:7

At a critical moment in His life, Jesus turned His face toward Jerusalem, where He would face betrayal, arrest, interrogation, persecution, torture, and death. Before He began this final journey, Jesus took Peter, James, and John up a mountain. There His appearance began to radiate with a brilliant light, from the inside out. Then the cloud of the Father's glory descended, and from deep within a voice began to speak. Just as at His baptism Jesus had heard the Father telling Him how much He loved Him, so now at His transfiguration Jesus heard the Father's loving affirmation once again, only this time with an additional command to the disciples—"listen to Him." This shows that the revelation of the Father's love was the most important resource in Jesus' life. It was this revelation that helped Him to face the devil in the desert. It was this that enabled him to endure the horrors of Calvary. This is an abiding lesson to all of us. We must keep our focus on the Father's love and be sustained by our sonship, not by our successes.

PRAYER

*Dearest Father, help me each and every day to hear
Your voice saying over me that I am Your child, marked
by Your love. In Jesus' name. Amen.*

Safe With My Father

"I and the Father are one heart and mind."
—JOHN 10:30

There are so many people who have had very negative experiences of being fathered. Maybe their father was abusive or addicted. Maybe he was absent or authoritarian. When a person with this sort of background comes to know Jesus, it is very often difficult for them to call God "Father." When they think of God in this way, they are reminded of how their own dads were, or are, with them. However, we must understand that when we get Jesus, we get the Father too. We cannot have a relationship with Jesus but neglect or reject the Father. No, when we come to Jesus, we come to the Father, because Jesus shows us the Father! More than that, Jesus and the Father are one, so you can't encounter one without encountering both! The key then is to allow the Holy Spirit to heal the wounds from our earthly fathers so that we can learn to know the true Father—the Father who never abandons or abuses His children. That way, we can truly learn to love the Father we've been waiting for all our lives.

PRAYER

Dear Lord Jesus, help me to understand that You reveal the Father heart of God, and that if I feel safe with You, I can feel safe with my Father too. Amen.

Call No Man Father

"No one else should carry the title of 'Father';
you have only one Father, and he's in heaven."
—MATTHEW 23:9

We have a very unhealthy tendency to put people on a pedestal. This is true in the world where celebrities are idolized. But it is also true in the Church as well. We have a tendency to imitate the world by elevating certain leaders and teachers to a level where they are objects of adulation. This is what was going on in Jesus' day. Many were admiring people who had a great gift of teaching. They were addressing them as "Teacher." Others were admiring people of great wisdom. They were being called "Father." Still others were admiring charismatic personalities. They were being called "Leader." Jesus warned us against doing this. As soon as a gifted human being is put on a pedestal it's not long before they are taking God's place in people's hearts. Only God should be worshipped as "Teacher." Only God should be adored as "Father." Only God should be regarded as "Leader." When we give to a human being the position that belongs to God alone, we are in deep trouble.

PRAYER

Lord Jesus, help me to reserve the title "Father" for God
alone. He is my true Abba Father. He is the One I love
and adore. In Your name. Amen.

Father's House

"There is plenty of room for you in my Father's home."
—JOHN 14:2

This is one of the most comforting promises in the Bible. Jesus is speaking to His disciples the night before He dies and is keen for them not to feel troubled. He tells them that there is plenty of room in His Father's house. What did He mean by that? In the original language, Jesus tells His followers that there are many rooms. He is talking about life after death, and He is reassuring them that there is a mansion in Heaven with more rooms than they could ever count. He is about to leave them, but death will not hold Him down. He is going to defeat death by being raised on the third day, and then He will return to Heaven where He will prepare rooms for His friends in His Father's house. What a great consolation that was for them, and what a great consolation it is for all of us. Let's never forget. Death for the child of God is not a hopeless end, but an endless hope. We get to live forever in the mansion of our Father, enjoying His love, dwelling for eternity in His life-giving presence.

PRAYER

Father, when I am troubled by the prospect of death,
renew my vision of Your eternal home, and my room in
the mansion of Your presence. Amen.

The Only Way

> "I am the Road, also the Truth, also the Life.
> No one gets to the Father apart from me."
> —JOHN 14:6

Jesus is saying three important things here. He is first of all the only Road to the Father. Second, He alone tells us the Truth about the Father. Third, He alone brings us the Life of the Father. Please notice the little word "the." Jesus does not say that He is "a" road, "a" truth, "a" life among many. When it comes to finding your way to *Abba* Father, when it comes to knowing the truth about *Abba* Father, when it comes to enjoying the life that flows from *Abba* Father, Jesus is the only source. There may be other roads on offer, other systems of truth, other sources of life—but when it comes to knowing God as *Father,* you cannot do that apart from Jesus. In a world that wants to relegate Jesus to just one way among many, we must be unashamed about the uniqueness of Jesus.

PRAYER

Jesus, I worship You that You alone provide the way to the Father. Help me to be fearless in standing up for Your uniqueness. In Your name. Amen.

Finding Contentment

"Show us the Father; then we'll be content."
—JOHN 14:8

Why is it so important to know the Father's love in our hearts? The answer is provided in the words of one of Jesus' disciples. Philip said, "Show us the Father; *then we'll be content*." Jesus replies by saying that Philip has already seen the Father because Jesus reveals the Father. In that sense, Philip had missed the point. He had failed to see that Jesus is the one and only Son who shows us what our Father is truly like. In another sense, however, Philip didn't miss the point. He understood that the person who receives a revelation of the Father finds true satisfaction in life. As he put it, "then we'll be *content*." Many Christians enjoy salvation but they do not necessarily experience satisfaction. Our hearts are only fully satisfied in the Father's love. Let's press in to the deep contentment of knowing God as Father.

PRAYER

Thank You, Jesus, for revealing that God is my loving Father. I ask You to reveal more of this truth so that my heart may be truly content. Amen.

Father's Words

"The words that I speak to you aren't mere words. I don't just make them up on my own. The Father who resides in me crafts each word into a divine act."
—John 14:10

Jesus is continuing His discussion with Philip, who has asked Him, "Show us the Father." Jesus tells Philip that the person who sees Jesus has seen the Father. More than that, everyone who hears Jesus speak has heard the Father too. What this shows is that everything Jesus did reveals the Father and everything He said reveals the Father too. Whenever Jesus spoke—whether it was in commands that healed the sick or in parables that entranced the crowds—He was speaking not His own words, but the words that His Father was telling Him to say. The Father was behind every statement Jesus ever uttered, crafting each word into a divine act. That's why whenever Jesus spoke, miraculous things happened. Hearts were changed. Sicknesses were healed. Death was defeated. Demons were cast out and storms were stilled. When Jesus spoke, people around Him were touched and the world around Him was affected. When Jesus opened His mouth, Heaven came to earth.

PRAYER

Dear Lord Jesus, I want to give You praise that Your words contain the life-changing power of Your Father and mine. In Your name. Amen.

Heart to Heart

"I am in my Father and my Father is in me."
—JOHN 14:11

If we have chosen to follow Jesus, then the goal of our entire lives is to walk like Jesus, think like Jesus, talk like Jesus and act like Jesus. What was it that marked Jesus out from everyone else, both in His own day and throughout history? It is this one single fact: that He could say, "I am in my Father and my Father is in me." If we want to draw closer to the Father heart of God, then we must make it our aim to be like Jesus and to live every waking moment of our lives "in our Father"—in other words, in the presence of the Father's love. More than that, we must make sure that not only do we live in the Father's heart but the Father lives in our hearts as well. We can do this because Jesus has died for our sins and removed the barrier that separated us from the Father's love. With the help of the Holy Spirit, we can now be at one with our Father, just as He is at one with us. Let's make it our aim to live in the Father's love and to let the Father live in us.

PRAYER

Dear Jesus, teach me to be like You, and to live in the heart of the Father's presence. Help me to know the Father's presence in my heart too. Amen.

Orphans No More

"I will not leave you orphaned."
—JOHN 14:18

The night before He died, Jesus told His disciples that He would not leave them as orphans. What did He mean? He cannot have been speaking literally, because some of the disciples had fathers who were still alive. The word "orphan" in the Bible means someone who is fatherless. That did not apply at a literal level. Jesus was therefore speaking figuratively. In a spiritual sense, all the disciples at this stage were orphans. They were still separated from their Father in Heaven because of sin. The next day, however, Jesus would die on the Cross and the barrier of sin would be destroyed. The disciples would no longer live as spiritual orphans. Putting their trust in Jesus and in the finished work of the Cross, they would able to know the Father's love in their hearts. All of us are orphans without Jesus, but when we are born again, we are no longer fatherless—we are Abba's children.

PRAYER

Thank You, Jesus for this great promise. I pray that You will help me to go from being an orphan to being Abba Father's child. In Your name. Amen.

At Home in My Heart

*"If anyone loves me, he will carefully keep
my word and my Father will love him—we'll
move right into the neighborhood!"*
—JOHN 14:23

When a person chooses to repent of their sins and put their trust in Jesus, they are born again. When that happens, a whole new life begins for them. They are no longer spiritual orphans. They become the adopted sons and daughters of God. When that happens, they commit to an entire lifetime of becoming more and more like Jesus. As adopted sons and daughters, our greatest dream is to become the best son or daughter we can be. That means doing everything that Jesus commands us to do. When we live like this, Jesus promises that we will know the Father's love. We will experience the Father moving into the neighborhood of our hearts, taking up residence in our lives, making His home in us, even as we make our home in Him. Let's make it our daily goal to be careful to keep Jesus' word, so that we may know the love of our Father.

PRAYER

*Abba, Father, help me to learn to be more obedient to
Your Son in my life, so that I may be more aware of
Your love in my heart. In Jesus' name. Amen.*

Our Goal and Purpose

"The Father is the goal and purpose of my life."
—JOHN 14:28

What does it mean to make the Father the goal and purpose of our lives? It means making sure that our primary aim every day is to know the Father more clearly—to have a keener sense of His nearness to us and our dearness to Him. It also means making sure that we don't order our lives on our own terms and according to our own dreams, but rather align our life's purpose to the Father's plan for our lives. In short, it means daily prioritizing the Father's intimacy and the Father's destiny. If everyone who professes to know Jesus could live by this rule of life, there would be revival throughout the globe. Too often we let our love for the Father wane; too often we don't put Him first and we drift into living life our own way. Let's ask the Holy Spirit to give us a fresh passion for making the Father the goal and purpose of our lives.

PRAYER

Dearest Father, don't let my love for You grow cold, and don't let me pursue my own dreams. Help me to know You intimately, and to seize Your destiny. Amen.

Father's Instructions

*"I am carrying out my Father's instructions
right down to the last detail."*
—JOHN 14:31

If we want to be obedient sons and daughters of God, then we will need to imitate Jesus, the one and only Son of God by nature. With the help of the Holy Spirit, Jesus in His human flesh carried out the Father's instructions right down to the last detail. All this is immensely encouraging, because it means that Jesus has given us an example of what we can accomplish too. We can resolve to be like Jesus, and in our human flesh receive the Father's blueprint for our lives and obey it to the letter, with the help of the same Holy Spirit. Let's delve deep into the Word of God together in these devotions and ask the Holy Spirit to help us to know with greater precision the Father's plan and purpose for our lives. Then let's make it our mission not just to be good starters, but to be good finishers too, just like Jesus.

PRAYER

Dear Lord Jesus, help me to know and then to obey the Father's instructions, and help me not to do that in a vague but in a rigorous way. Amen.

Balanced Theology

"I am the Real Vine and my Father is the Farmer."
—JOHN 15:1

It is so important to have a balanced understanding of the Father heart of God. Some people veer too far toward a sentimental extreme, portraying God as a Daddy who will condone almost any behavior. And then there are those who veer too far towardsa judgmental extreme, portraying God as a wrathful Father, who excludes and punishes all but a few. The truth, as so often is the case, lies in the radical middle. God is our loving Father, yes, but He loves us far too much to let us stay as we have been, bound by our sins and hurts. This is the point Jesus is making in His teaching about the True Vine. Here Jesus talks about us as branches on a vine. God is our Farmer as well as our Father. He comes and tends to these branches, pruning what is unproductive from our lives, cutting us back so that we can be fruitful in the future. We should always remember this. Our Father wants us to be holy, and He wants us to be whole, just like His Son Jesus. Let's welcome the Farmer's knife because the knife brings life!

PRAYER

Dearest Father, I submit to Your refining process today.
Lead me into greater holiness and wholeness, so that I
can be truly fruitful. In Jesus' name. Amen.

A True Reflection

"This is how my Father shows who He is—when you
produce grapes, when you mature as my disciples."
—JOHN 15:8

Jesus declares that He is the True Vine. In His day, the Jewish
people saw themselves as the vine of God. Jesus tells them that
He is the real vine. What counts is no longer being a part of a
nation but being a part of Him. Those who commit to a life of
growing maturity in the Father's love are like fruitful branches.
They go deep in intimacy and extend far and wide in productivity. Only those who are prepared to submit to the gardener's
pruning knife and have their hurts, habits and hang ups dealt
with will bear lasting fruit. Those who say "yes" to this lifelong
process, grow up to become mature sons and daughters of God
and productive disciples of Christ. In this, our Father reveals who
He truly is. He is not just a Father who wants to embrace us, He
is also a Farmer who wants to transform us. Let's show the world
what kind of Father God truly is by letting Him change us so
that we are more like Jesus every day.

PRAYER

*Dearest Father, I want to be a true reflection of who
You really are. Help me to say "yes" to the refining and
maturing process in my life. In Jesus' name. Amen.*

Love~Based Holiness

"I've loved you the way my Father has loved
me. Make yourselves at home in my love."
—JOHN 15:9

There is no love like the Father's love. It is deeper than the deepest ocean and higher than the highest heavens. Jesus lived in that love every day of His life on earth. Jesus tells His disciples that this is how He has loved them as well. He has poured out His love upon them, being patient with their imperfections and forbearing with their failures. He now invites them to make their home in this divine love for the rest of their lives. He does not invite them to make their home in religion—in a system of rules and regulations. He invites them to make their home in relationship—in the closest possible intimacy with the Father. The primary characteristic of those who make their home in this holy love is that they seek to become more and more obedient to God. This is not a law-based holiness, such as we find in religion. It is a love-based obedience, such as we find in relationship with Jesus. Let's make ourselves at home in the Father's holy love.

PRAYER

Father, deliver me from law-based holiness into love-based obedience. Help me to want to do what You want me to do, because of Your great love. Amen.

Slaves No More

"I'm no longer calling you servants because servants don't understand what their master is thinking and planning. No, I've named you friends because I've let you in on everything I've heard from the Father."
—John 15:15

It is the night before He will die, and Jesus is preparing His disciples for the time of His return to the Father. He shares with them that an epic transition is now taking place. Up until this point the disciples have been the servants of God (the word literally means "slaves"). Now, however, they are going to become God's friends. What is the difference? Servants relate to God as a slave does to a Master. Consequently, they do not have access to God's heart. They are not in on His plans. Friends, on the other hand, live very close to the Father's heart because of what Jesus has done for them on the Cross. They are in on everything the Father says. Which kind of relationship with God do you want? Do you want to be a slave or a son? Do you want to be a servant or a friend? When you make the transition from a slave-Master relationship to a son-Father relationship, you begin to enjoy the benefits that Jesus paid for on the Cross.

PRAYER

Dearest Father, help me not to relate to You as a slave to a Master, but as a child to a Father, and as a friend to Jesus. Help me to live close to Your heart. Amen.

True Alignment

*"As fruit bearers, whatever you ask the
Father in relation to me, he gives you."*
—JOHN 15:16

One of the great blessings of the Cross is that we no longer relate to God as a remote deity, but as a relational Dad. This means that we can talk with Him about anything at any time. More than that, we can also make requests as well. What Jesus is talking about here is prayer. When we are truly abiding in Jesus, then we know Jesus' heart. We are completely in tune with His nature. When that happens, we approach our Father in prayer and make requests. We do this "in the name of Jesus." In Jesus' day, the name of a person was the same as the character of a person. To pray for something in Jesus' name means to ask for something that is in alignment with His character. It is to ask what Jesus would ask in any given situation. When we do that, Jesus promises that the Father will give it to us. Let's be so at one with Jesus that we ask what He would ask and receive what He would receive from our Father in Heaven.

PRAYER

*Lord Jesus, help me to be so at one with You that my
prayers are Your prayers. Help me always to pray in
alignment with Your will. In Your name. Amen.*

The Father's Friend

"When the Friend I plan to send you from the Father comes—the Spirit of Truth issuing from the Father—he will confirm everything about me."
—JOHN 15:26

The night before Jesus dies, He tells His disciples that He will not leave them as orphans—as people separated from the Father's love. He will come back to them when He is raised from the dead. More than that, after He has returned home to the Father, He is going to send the Holy Spirit to be their Friend. This Friend will live forever in their hearts. This Friend will be so full of truth that the disciples will consistently know what is true about God from what is false. This Friend will therefore also confirm everything that Jesus said and did, proving that He was and is the only Son of God, the Savior of the World, the Lord of lords, the King of kings, and the Alpha and the Omega—the Beginning and the End. Aren't you grateful that we are not only called to be the friends of God, we are also equipped by the Friend that issues out of the heart of the Father?

PRAYER

Dearest Father, help me to know more deeply in my heart the presence of the Friend who confirms everything about Your Son Jesus. In His name. Amen.

Paying the Price

"They never really understood the Father."
—JOHN 16:3

There are those who grasp that God is our loving Father, and there are those who do not. Those who fail to understand the Father often end up hating God's true children with a passion. This hatred stems from an inability to grasp the fact that Jesus was and is the only Son of God by nature, who came to reveal the Father. Never forget that those who do not know the Father operate with a completely different worldview. This worldview is clouded by a deep and dark deception that comes from the devil, the father of lies. The devil wants to keep people separated from the Father's love. That is His plan. To do this, he keeps people blind to the true nature of God, and moves them to hate God's children with a passion. This hatred can come from within the religious community just as much as from without. That is why Jesus warns His followers that they will even be thrown out of places of worship (synagogues) for their faith in Jesus. Truly understanding the Father is a matter of life and death.

PRAYER

Dear God, help me to continue to grow in my understanding of Your fatherly heart, and to be prepared to pay the price for this great revelation. Amen.

The Incredible Journey

"First, I left the Father and arrived in the world;
now I leave the world and travel to the Father."
—JOHN 16:28

Jesus' story did not begin in a manger then come to an end at His death. Rather, it began in Heaven before He was even born. It began with Jesus saying to His Father in eternity, "I am willing to go to this orphaned planet called Earth and die so that people may be able to know you as Father!" It came to an end with Jesus being raised from the dead and returning home to the glorious presence of His Father in Heaven. We should never forget that Jesus Christ, as the only Son of God by nature, chose to leave the majesty of His Father's presence in Heaven to come to our world in order to rescue us. We should never forget that, after He fulfilled all that the Father had asked Him to do, Jesus returned to an unparalleled homecoming in which the whole of Heaven stood to applaud Him for completing the Father's mission. What an extraordinary journey that is, and all for our sakes!

PRAYER

Dear Lord Jesus, thank You for the true story that
You came from the Father's presence in Heaven and
returned to Your Father at Your ascension. Amen.

Never Alone

"I'm not abandoned. The Father is with me."
—JOHN 16:32

What a truly wonderful thing to say! Jesus is about to walk the Calvary Road and die for the sins of the world. He is about to be deserted by His friends and vilified by His enemies. If ever there was an outcast, it was Jesus. If ever there was a man on His own, it was Him. But Jesus says this: "It's going to look as if the whole world's walked out on me. But don't you worry—I stand with a Father who never leaves or forsakes me. He will be with me through thick and thin, come hell or high water." It doesn't matter how dire our circumstances become, the truth is we can say this too. If we know that God is our loving, ever-faithful Father, then we also know that He has promised never to walk out on us and leave us solitary and deserted. As the adopted sons and daughters of God, we can make the same decree as the Son by nature. "I'm not abandoned. The Father is with me." Hallelujah! What a Father!

PRAYER

*Dearest Father, I thank You that You stand with me
even if everyone else has seemed to desert me, and that I
will never be alone. In Jesus' name. Amen.*

God's Timing

"Father, it's time."
—JOHN 17:1

We have seen already in these devotions how Jesus lived in such intimate communion with His Father that He only ever did what He saw His Father doing. Nowhere is this more the case than in Jesus' return home. Throughout John's Gospel this is referred to as "the hour." Jesus has in mind an hour in which He is going to go back home to His Father. This is not a literal 60 minutes, but a timeframe encompassing everything involved in Jesus being "lifted up." This includes the crucifixion, when Jesus is hoisted onto a Roman cross, and the resurrection, when Jesus is raised up from death. It also includes Jesus' ascension, when He is lifted up to Heaven, and His session, in which He sits down at the right hand of the Father, having completed His work. This is an hour that changed the history of the world. Thanks to Jesus' obedience, we who were once spiritual orphans will now have the opportunity of enjoying intimate communion with the Father as well. We too will be able to say at the strategic moments of our lives, "Father, it's time."

PRAYER

Father, I thank You that You have a plan for my life, and that You want me to fulfill it in Your time. Help me to be in sync with Your timing. Amen.

The Central Revelation

"I have made your very being known to them."
—JOHN 17:26

In John 17, Jesus is praying to His Father and saying, "I have revealed who You truly are to my disciples." What is it that Jesus has made known? It is the fact that God is our Father. Yes, God is Creator, Redeemer, Deliverer, and so much more, but all of these things arise from a deeper revelation still—that God is the most loving Father of all. This is the central revelation of Jesus Christ. If Jesus hadn't come to us and shown us this, we would never have known. Be thankful that He has revealed that Almighty God is the world's greatest Father. Be grateful that He continues to make this known to people like you and me. If you don't know God as your loving Father, ask Jesus to help you to experience the Father's embrace. He wants us to know His love, not just as doctrine in our heads, but as an experience in our hearts.

PRAYER

Dear Lord Jesus, I cannot thank You enough for making the Father's heart known. Please help me to experience this in my heart. In Your name. Amen.

A Deepening Intimacy

"And continue to make it known...."
—John 17:26

It is very important to understand that the revelation of the Father wasn't restricted to Jesus' ministry two thousand years ago. No, Jesus promised in John 17 that He would *continue* to make the Father known. This is great news! Jesus Christ is still revealing the Father today! Notice that He promises to continue to make the Father *known*. The word "know" is an important one. It doesn't refer to intellectual knowledge. It refers to personal, intimate, relational knowledge. I can write about the Father's love and you will know about it, but this is not true knowledge. Jesus wants us to experience the Father in our hearts, not just assent to the fact that He is our Father in our heads. Thank God that we can encounter the Father's love today! We do this by believing what the Bible says about the Father's love for us and by walking in the Spirit of adoption, who witnesses in our spirits (the deepest part of our being) that we are the children of God.

PRAYER

Dear Lord Jesus, please make the Father known to my heart, so that I can truly experience a deepening intimacy with the living God. In Your name. Amen.

No Greater Love

"So that your love for me might be in them...."
—JOHN 17:26

I'd like to invite you to consider for a moment the love of the Father for His Son, Jesus Christ. It is a love that is higher than the highest heavens and deeper than the deepest oceans. It is a love beyond all imagining. Jesus walked in this love every day and every night of His life here on this Earth. But there is something even more wonderful than this. In John 17 Jesus is communicating with His Father in prayer. He tells His Father that He has made Him known and will continue to do so. Why? Here's the marvel and the mystery—so that the love that the Father has for the Son might be in us too. Did you notice the little word "in"? Jesus prays that we would have a burning fire deep within our hearts—the fire of the Father's love for Jesus. What a privilege this is! We too can revel in the Father's love for Jesus. We too can know the Love of all loves. All we have to do is make sure we find our heart's true home in the Father's love and rest in this reality every day.

PRAYER

Dear Father, help me to experience in the very core of my being that same love that You forever have for Your one and only Son. In His name. Amen.

Doing Abba's Will

"Papa, Father, you can—can't you?—get me
out of this. Take this cup away from me."
—MARK 14:35

Jesus is in Gethsemane the night before He dies. He comes before God in anguish about the cup He is about to drink. As he agonizes over the impending ordeal of Calvary, He calls God "Papa, Father." The word "Papa" is a translation of the word, "Abba." If you go to Israel and you're invited into a Jewish home, you will often see children playing with their dads and calling out *Abba*. In Hebrew, *Abba* means "Daddy" and *Imma* means "Mummy." Yes, there is honor in these words, but they are also terms of endearment. They denote intimate relationship not distant regard. When Jesus prayed, He called the God of the Universe His *Abba*. He asked His Dearest Father to make it possible for Him not to have to go through the agony of crucifixion. He knew that His Father had the power to do this, but He also said, "Nevertheless, Your will be done." This shows that being a true son is not just a matter of knowing the Father's heart. It's about doing the Father's perfect will.

PRAYER

*Dear Lord Jesus, teach me by Your Holy Spirit not only
to enjoy the Father's heart but also to obey the Father's
will for my life. In Your name. Amen.*

The True Son

> With the crowd before him, Pilate said, "Which
> prisoner do you want me to pardon: Jesus
> Barabbas, or Jesus the so-called Christ?"
> —MATTHEW 27:17

Jesus is arrested and taken before the Roman governor Pontius Pilate who knows that Jesus is innocent. He therefore tries to find a way out by seizing upon a so-called Passover amnesty. He tells the crowds they have a choice. They can either release a well-known insurgent called Jesus Barabbas, or they can have Jesus—an innocent man—set free. See what a grim irony there is right here! What does the name *Barabbas* mean? If you look, you can see two words, *Bar* and *Abba*. *Bar* means son and *Abba* means Father. Although Abbas might have been the actual name of this bandit's father, there is a terrible coincidence in the word play. The guilty man has a name that sounds as near as possible to "Son of my Father." The innocent man is the one and only Son of the Father in Heaven. The crowd opts to have the wrong Jesus released. The One who truly reveals the Father is condemned. The enemy of Rome is set free—a great error of judgment on Pilate's part.

PRAYER

Father, I declare that there is only one man who deserves to be called the Son of the Father by nature, Your Son Jesus, in His mighty name. Amen.

A New Family

He said to his mother, "Woman, here is your son."
Then to the disciple, "Here is your mother."
—JOHN 19:26–27

As Jesus struggles for breath on the Cross, he looks down at those supporting Him in His final hours on the earth. There is His mother Mary, weeping at the terrible death her son is enduring. And there is the beloved disciple, whom church tradition has commonly associated with John—the author of the Gospel of John. Before He dies, Jesus turns to them and tells them that they now belong to each other, mother and son. This is a beautiful gesture. Not only is Jesus ensuring that His mother is going to have someone look after her, but He also effectively adopts the beloved disciple into His family. This is a picture of what Jesus has achieved for all of us. Through the blood that He shed, He bought us out of slavery and adopted us into His Father's family. When Jesus creates this new family at His bruised feet, He creates a picture of what He has done for all of us. If we love Jesus, we are all adopted into the Father's family.

PRAYER

Thank You so much, Jesus, for creating a new family at the Cross, and for choosing me to be a son, a daughter, of my Father in Heaven. Amen.

Father, Where Are You?

> At three o'clock, Jesus groaned out of the
> depths, crying loudly, "Eloi, Eloi, lama
> sabachthani?" which means, "My God, my
> God, why have you abandoned me?"
> —MARK 15:34

At Calvary Jesus breaks from His normal practice of referring to God as His Father, and honors the original words of Psalm 22, crying, "My God, my God, why have you abandoned me?" We might ask at this point, how can this be? Did Jesus not say that His Father never abandoned Him? Here we must distinguish between what was true in reality and what Jesus felt in His humanity. In reality, the Father, the Son and the Holy Spirit were in unbroken unity at Calvary. At the same time, *in His humanity* Jesus felt for the first and only time an agonizing sense of His Father's absence. Having taken our sin in His body, Jesus experienced the consequence of sin—separation from His Father. This is love—in His human heart, the Son experienced for a moment what it was like to be a spiritual orphan, so that we who are spiritual orphans might become God's daughters and sons. Maybe you have sometimes asked, "Father, where are you?" If you have, be reassured—Jesus understands.

PRAYER

Lord Jesus, thank You that You endured a crushing
sense of separation from the Father so that we could
come home to the Father's arms of love. Amen.

Father, Forgive

Jesus prayed, "Father, forgive them; they
don't know what they're doing."
—LUKE 23:34

These are extraordinarily powerful words. Who is Jesus speaking about? He is referring to the quaternion (the squad of four men) at the foot of the Cross, the Roman legionaries who are executing Him. They would have performed this duty numerous times. They have no idea that the man they are now crucifying is the Father's one and only Son. Jesus looks down on them, and the others standing in the crowd, and sees them through the eyes of an extraordinary, divine mercy. Who is He talking to? He is speaking to the One whom He addressed as His *Abba*, His Heavenly Father. He is appealing to the Father's heart, which is a heart of extreme compassion. What is He asking for? He is praying that His Father will not hold this sin against them because they are ignorant of the true significance of their acts. What a beautiful picture this is. Here, at the Cross, we see the Son communing in an intimate way with His Father, releasing forgiveness to those who don't deserve it.

PRAYER

Dearest Father, I have sinned many times—willfully as well as unwittingly. Please release the forgiveness of the Cross into my life. Amen.

Into the Night

Jesus called loudly, "Father, I place my life in
your hands!" Then he breathed his last.
—LUKE 23:46

Every Jewish child was taught by their parents to say a prayer at
night before they went to sleep. This prayer was based on Psalm
31:5, where King David prayed, "Into Your hands I commit my
spirit" (NIV). This was the prayer that Jesus would have prayed
as a boy when He was growing up in his parent's home. Now, as
He gasps His last breaths, He prays this same prayer again. As
Jesus falls asleep in death, He makes a great statement of faith.
He declares that His spirit is now in the hands of His Father in
Heaven. Just as Jesus woke up every morning after praying that
prayer every night, so He trusts in His heart that He will wake up
on the first Easter morning, just as He fell asleep on Good Friday.
What a great example Jesus has left us. We could do no better
than saying this every night before we go to sleep. We could do
no better than saying this with resurrection faith at the end of
our lives.

PRAYER

*Dearest Father, I give You praise that my life is in Your
perfect hands—my sleeping and waking, my dying and
rising. In Jesus' name. Amen.*

The Son of God

When the Roman captain standing guard in
front of him saw that he had quit breathing,
he said, "This has to be the Son of God!"
—MARK 15:39

We saw in a previous devotion how Jesus asked His Father to forgive the soldiers around the Cross because they had no idea of the significance of their actions. However, the centurion in charge of the executing party was different. He saw the way that Jesus died, and something in his heart began to change, so much so that he declared that Jesus had to be the Son of God. This was truly radical. In Jesus' day, there was only one person who was declared "son of god," and that was the Roman emperor. He was called "son of god," "lord," "savior of the world," by every citizen in the Roman Empire. But the emperor was just a man who decided he wanted to become a god. Jesus, on the other hand, was God, who decided He wanted to become a man. More than that, He was the Lord of lords and the true Savior of the World. This is what the centurion glimpsed. This is the daring proclamation he uttered. Here, a non-Jewish, pagan soldier recognizes that Jesus, not Caesar, is truly the Father's Son.

PRAYER

*Dear Lord Jesus, I agree! You are truly the only one in
history who deserves to be called the Son of God, Lord of
lords, and Savior of the World. Amen.*

A Death-Defeating Dad

Mary Magdalene came to the tomb and saw that
the stone was moved away from the entrance.
—JOHN 20:1

The Bible tells us that on the third day, Jesus rose from the dead. Keep in mind that for the Jewish people a day started at 6PM and ended 24 hours later at 6PM. Jesus died on Good Friday afternoon (Day 1). Day 2 began Friday evening at 6PM. Day 3 began at 6PM on Saturday evening. At some point very early in the morning during that third day, something absolutely momentous happened. Jesus was dead and buried in the tomb. A massive, one-ton stone was rolled against the entrance. Then suddenly the Father acted. The power of the Holy Spirit burst into the tomb and into Jesus' dead body. Jesus woke up, fully alive! The stone was then moved as if it weighed nothing, as Jesus left. Consequently, when Mary Magdalene arrived she found the tomb empty and the grave clothes of Jesus folded neatly within. What a glorious, history-making and world-changing moment. What an all-powerful Father we have as well! Our Father is a death-defeating, grave-busting Father! Thanks to Him, Jesus is alive!

PRAYER

*Dearest Father, I worship You that You raised Your Son
Jesus from the dead and that You revealed Your glory
when the stone was rolled away. Amen.*

Fatherly Vindication

His unique identity as Son of God was shown by
the Spirit when Jesus was raised from the dead.
—ROMANS 1:4

When Jesus was raised from the dead, it changed everything, especially our understanding of who Jesus was. Up until then, it would have been possible for someone to say that Jesus was an exceptionally holy man, a miracle worker, and a man of unusual compassion. In other words, it might have been possible for a skeptical person to say that Jesus was a prophet, but not the one and only Son of God by nature. After the resurrection, this was no longer possible. On the third day, our Father proved that Jesus was His only Son by raising Him from the dead through the power of the Holy Spirit. The resurrection of Jesus was therefore the Father's vindication and validation of Jesus' own claim to be the Father's Son. It was a final and irrefutable confirmation of Jesus' divine identity. From now on, people must make a decision about Jesus. Either He was just a great man who died a terrible death, or He was the Son of God who paid for our sins and conquered the grave.

PRAYER

Dearest Father, I thank You for sending Your Spirit on the third day to raise Jesus. Thank You for proving that He was and is Your Son. Amen.

My Father and Yours

> "Go to my brothers and tell them, 'I ascend to my
> Father and your Father, my God and your God.'"
> —JOHN 20:17

On the third day after His death, Jesus was raised and the stone rolled away from the mouth of His tomb. He walked out into the dawn of a new day and a new age. Mary Magdalene, who loved Him dearly, was still lingering at the tomb, weeping at the death of the rabbi and friend who had set her free. But then her tears of sorrow were turned to tears of joy. Jesus appeared to her and told her that He was returning to His Father in Heaven. He gave her a message to take to the disciples who were cowering behind a locked door in Jerusalem for fear of the Jewish leaders. He told her to let them know that He was ascending to His Father and *to their Father*. Notice that God is now their Father too! Up until this point, the disciples have not known this in their hearts. Now Jesus has removed the sin that separated them from the Father's love. Now God is their Abba too! Truly a new age has begun— the Age of the Father's Love.

PRAYER

*Dear Lord Jesus, thank You for removing the barrier of
sin and opening up a way back home into the Father's
arms of love. In Your name. Amen.*

Waiting

> He told them that they were on no
> account to leave Jerusalem but "must
> wait for what the Father promised."
> —ACTS 1:4

There were 120 disciples by the time the Day of Pentecost came. These disciples met with the Risen Jesus in the days before He returned to His Father in Heaven. Jesus made it clear to them that it was to their advantage that He was leaving. While He was on the earth, the Holy Spirit was restricted to where Jesus was in His human body. Once He ascended to Heaven, however, He could pour out the Father's promised gift of the Holy Spirit on everyone who chose to believe in Him. When Jesus left, the disciples stayed in Jerusalem and waited for the Father's promise. Waiting did not mean idle passivity. In the Bible, waiting is active and intentional. It involves a passionate pursuit of what the Father has promised. It requires a decision to go on believing in what you cannot yet see, until you see the thing for which you have believed. This is what the disciples did. They pursued the presence of God until it became manifest in their hearts and their midst on the Day of Pentecost.

PRAYER

Dearest Father, I thank You that You have promised the Holy Spirit to all those who put their trust in Jesus. I believe. Help me to receive! Amen.

O Happy Day!

"You don't get to know the time.
Timing is the Father's business."
—ACTS 1:7

During the 40 days between Jesus' resurrection and ascension, He taught His disciples about the Kingdom of God. Inevitably, discussion turned to when this Kingdom would be fully established on the earth. This question, related to the Second Coming of Christ, fascinates the followers of Jesus even to this day. Jesus' answer is very telling. He says that the exact date and hour is up to the Father, and Him alone. In Jewish marriage customs during the New Testament era, the bridegroom would propose to the bride-to-be, then, if the answer was yes, he would return to his father's house to build new rooms. When the father deemed it ready, and the timing right, he would say to his son, "You may go and fetch your bride, bring her home and consummate the marriage." The father's decision was final. So it is with our Father in Heaven. He is the one who says "It's time." No one else does. When that happens, the Bridegroom and the Bride will rejoice together. Oh what a happy day that will be!

PRAYER

Dear Lord Jesus, help me not to get distracted by
speculations concerning the date of Your return. Help
me to trust that Father knows best. Amen.

Heaven's Family

"Go out and train everyone you meet, far and near,
in this way of life, marking them by baptism in the
threefold name: Father, Son, and Holy Spirit."
—MATTHEW 28:19

Just before Jesus returned to His Father in Heaven, He instructed His followers to go out to the peoples of every nation and to make disciples. When such unbelievers came to faith, He told His followers to baptize them in water and to do so in the name of "the Father, Son and Holy Spirit." Here we see Jesus speaking very clearly about what we now refer to as the Trinity. God is one being. That is a sacrosanct truth in both Judaism and Christianity. However, where Christianity departs from Judaism is in believing that God is three persons—Father, Son and Holy Spirit—while never ceasing to be one being. God is a divine family of three persons who co-exist in one being or nature. When a person becomes a Christian, they are baptized in the name of this divine family. Indeed, they become a part of the Father's family here on earth. Let's always celebrate the family of Heaven and resolve to create families of faith and love all over the earth.

PRAYER

*Dear Lord Jesus, help me to obey Your command to go
and make and baptize disciples. Help me to extend the
Father's family here on earth. Amen.*

The Promise Keeper

"Raised to the heights at the right hand of God and receiving the promise of the Holy Spirit from the Father, he poured out the Spirit he had just received!"
—ACTS 2:33

After 40 days, the risen Jesus ascends to heaven and returns to His father. There He receives the Holy Spirit whom the Father had promised, and then pours out the spirit upon the 120 disciples on the Day of Pentecost. This is a momentous moment. Up until this point, the Holy Spirit had not been given to the disciples. Jesus had promised that they would not be left as orphans—separated from the Father's love—but that they would receive the Holy Spirit to be in their hearts forever. What a promise this is! Maybe you had a father who didn't keep his promises. He said he would do something or give you something, but he didn't deliver. This led you to mistrust what he said. You need to know that this is absolutely not what our Heavenly Father is like. When He makes a promise, He always keeps it.

PRAYER

Dearest Father, I thank You that You keep Your promises. Thank You that You have embraced me with the Father's love. Amen.

An Unexpected Embrace

No sooner were these words out of Peter's mouth
than the Holy Spirit came on the listeners.
—ACTS 10:44

The Apostle Peter goes to the household of a Gentile centurion called Cornelius. He is not enthusiastic about this, but God shows Peter that He is a Father with no favorites. Peter obeys, and as he is sharing the Gospel, the Holy Spirit falls upon the Gentile audience. Notice a number of important things. First, it was while Peter is speaking that the Holy Spirit comes. God did not wait for Peter to make an appeal before He intervened! Second, the Holy Spirit comes upon those whom the Jews tried to avoid. Once again, this is a sign of the Father's inclusive heart. Third, Luke (who wrote the Book of Acts) says that the Holy Spirit "fell upon" the Gentiles. This is exactly the same verb that Luke uses in Luke 15:20 when the father falls upon the shoulders of his returning son. What's the lesson? It doesn't matter who you are or where you're from; when you say "yes" to the Good News about Jesus, the Holy Spirit falls upon you and you receive the affectionate embrace of your Father.

PRAYER

Dear Lord Jesus, help me to be a person who leads others to say yes to the Gospel, so that they too may receive the Father's embrace. In Your name. Amen.

Drenched in Love

He ordered that they be baptized
in the name of Jesus Christ.
—ACTS 10:48

In Acts 10, Peter sees something utterly remarkable: non-Jews are being filled with the Holy Spirit. Seeing that these "pagans" have been saved, Peter orders that each one of them should be baptized in water. The word baptism comes from a Greek word that means "drench" or "saturate." It is an intensive form of a verb meaning "dip." Just as these Gentiles had been baptized, or drenched, in the Holy Spirit, now they are baptized, or drenched, in water. This involved them going down into the water and then rising up out of the water. This was an outward and visible expression of an inward and invisible transition. In each and every case, these new disciples had gone from being dead in sin to being alive in Christ. They had gone from being slaves to sin to being the adopted sons and daughters of God. We should always place a very high value on water baptism. It is a public sign that we have said goodbye to death and hello to life, goodbye to slavery and hello to sonship.

PRAYER

Father, help me to understand baptism as a symbolic act in which a person dies to slavery and rises to sonship. In the name of Jesus. Amen.

Where Grace Reigns

Each of us is raised into a light-filled world
by our Father so that we can see where we're
going in our new grace-sovereign country.
—ROMANS 6:4

In the previous devotion we saw how Peter baptized Cornelius and his household in water. This was what the first Christians did. They preached the Good News about Jesus, and when people responded, four things happened: they repented of their sins, put their faith in Christ, received the gift of the Holy Spirit, and were baptized in water. Why did they need to be baptized in water? For the earliest Christians, as for believers today, baptism was understood as dying to our slavery to sin and rising to new life as an adopted son or daughter of God. In this respect it was an act of identification with the one and only Son by nature; He died and was buried but then was raised to new life. This is the point Paul makes in Romans 6. When we are baptized, it is like being buried with Christ and being raised with Christ. We say farewell to the old and we welcome the new. What is the new? It is the Father's gift to us: life lived in a light-filled world, a country where grace rules. Doesn't that sound good?

PRAYER

*Dearest Father, thank You so much for the amazing
beauty of the new life You have in store for all those who
go through the waters of baptism. Amen.*

Limitless Love

We can't round up enough containers to
hold everything God generously pours into
our lives through the Holy Spirit!
—ROMANS 5:5

In a previous devotion we saw in Acts 10 how the Holy Spirit fell upon the Gentiles just as the father fell upon the shoulders of the prodigal son. When a person says "yes" to the invitation to follow Jesus, the Father gives that person His affectionate embrace. Here in Romans 5:5, the Apostle Paul says something similar. There is simply no limit to the generosity of our Father when it comes to the giving of the Holy Spirit. When we say "yes" to Jesus, He pours out His love in our hearts through the Holy Spirit. Oh yes, the Holy Spirit is about power—the power to be effective witnesses that Jesus is alive. But the Holy Spirit is also about love. When a person is filled with the Spirit as they choose to believe in Christ, they are filled with the Father's amazing love. It is this love that empowers and motivates us to love the lost, the last and the least, just as Jesus did. Let's make sure that the container of our hearts is always filled with the Father's limitless love!

PRAYER

*Dear Father, I pray that You would pour out Your
Spirit in my heart with such generosity that I cannot
stop myself talking about Jesus. Amen.*

Always Expectant

This resurrection life you received from God is not a
timid, grave-tending life. It's adventurously expectant,
greeting God with a childlike "What's next, Papa?"
—ROMANS 8:15

A person walking in the presence of God is a person filled with
the life of Heaven. This life is not just something we long for
when we die. It is something we can enjoy now. With this death-
defeating, resurrection power at work within us, we no longer
find ourselves living a timid life. Rather we live adventurously.
We don't find ourselves living in a cemetery, always overseeing
death. We find ourselves in a nursery, always stewarding life.
When a person is walking in the presence of God, they greet
God with an expectant heart. They cry out, "What's next, Papa?"
When a person is filled with the Spirit of adoption, they are no
longer settlers; they are pioneers. Always remember, you have a
Father who calls you to be a risk-taker not an undertaker! You are
a son or a daughter of God by adoption. You are not a slave to
fear. Every day is an adventure with God as your Papa!

PRAYER

*Dearest Father, I want to wake up each day saying,
"What's next Papa?" Help me to be adventurously
expectant as an adopted child of God. Amen.*

Blessed Assurance

God's Spirit touches our spirits and confirms
who we really are. We know who He is, and
we know who we are: Father and children.
—ROMANS 8:16

When we come to know Jesus Christ, we receive the gift of the Holy Spirit. We are not left as orphans, separated from the Father's love. Once we repent of our sins and put our trust in Christ, then God fills us with the Holy Spirit. This enables us every day to live with total security about who we are. We no longer need constant reassuring. We have the Holy Spirit who tells us each moment that we are the adopted children of God. When that happens, we grow in our blessed assurance that God is our loving Heavenly Father and we are His dearly loved children. Let's therefore open up our lives at the level of our "spirits"— that deepest, spiritual part of our being—to the infinite love of the Father. Let's enjoy the continuous reminder and revelation of God's true identity—our Father; and our identity too—His beloved sons and daughters. Let's make sure that our security is in our position as God's children, not in our performance for Him.

PRAYER

*Dear Lord Jesus, I open up my spirit to Your Spirit
every day, so that I might know without any doubt that
God is my Papa and I am His child. Amen.*

Co~Heirs With Jesus

We know we are going to get what's coming
to us—an unbelievable inheritance!
—ROMANS 8:17

When boys were adopted in the days of the Apostle Paul, they were usually slaves or the sons of slaves. Most often the adopting father was a free man who owned an estate. He wanted a son but couldn't have one. Adoption was therefore his only solution. Once that adoption was complete, that boy's entire future was transformed. He was no longer bound by poverty. All his debts were cancelled and he found himself rich beyond anything he could have dreamed. More than that, no longer did he wake up with a sense of despair about the future. Now he woke up full of hope, because he knew that one day he would inherit everything his father owned. This is true of us too. Once we were impoverished slaves, with no hope. But now, thanks to Jesus, we are adopted sons and daughters, with a tremendous inheritance. We are one day going to inherit brand new resurrection bodies and we are going to inherit the earth! Let's rejoice in our unbelievable inheritance!

PRAYER

Dearest Father, I give You praise that as Your adopted child I am a co-heir with Jesus, and that one day I will inherit what He inherited. In His name. Amen.

The Pain and the Power

> If we go through the hard times with
> him, then we're certainly going to go
> through the good times with him!
> —ROMANS 8:17

In Romans 8, Paul teaches us that we are no longer slaves. We are the adopted sons and daughters of God. This does not mean we are the same as Jesus in nature. However, it does mean that we are like Jesus in calling, because the adopted children are meant to do what Jesus did. This inevitably means suffering from time to time. Like Jesus, we may have to endure persecution, perils and poverty. This should never surprise us. Nor should it ever depress or overwhelm us. This is, in fact, good news. If we endure hard times with Jesus, we will surely enjoy good times with Him too. If we partner with Him in His sufferings, we will surely partner with Him in encountering the glory of God in our lives. Let us never forget, our Heavenly Father is looking for sons and daughters who are prepared to experience what Jesus experienced—the pain as well as the power.

PRAYER

Dearest Father, help me to be prepared to embrace the suffering of the Cross, not just the glory of the Resurrection. Make me like Jesus, I pray. Amen.

Resting Not Striving

When the time arrived that was set by God
the Father, God sent his Son, born among
us of a woman, born under the conditions
of the law so that he might redeem those of
us who have been kidnapped by the law.
—GALATIANS 4:4–5

Right from the Garden of Eden, our Father had a rescue plan. He planned in advance to send His Son from Heaven to earth. This Son, Jesus Christ, would be born as a Jewish boy under the law. He would grow up and obey the law all the days of His life. Then, at the Cross, He would redeem those under the law. What does this mean? The picture here is of slavery. All of us were once slaves to the law. We tried to obey God's instructions, but we never measured up. Then Jesus came and He obeyed the law in every respect, and He did so with delight in His heart because He adored His Father. Consequently, He alone could pay the price to set us free from the slavery of always trying to earn the Father's acceptance. Through His blood, He set us free from this life of endless striving. We can now rest in the sure knowledge that the Father accepts us in His beloved Son—on the basis of our position, not our performance.

PRAYER

*Dearest Father, I cannot thank You enough that I no
longer have to strive to earn Your love. Thank You for
redeeming me from this life of law. Amen.*

A Father to All

God sent the Spirit of His Son into our
lives, crying out "Papa! Father!"
—GALATIANS 4:6

Here the Apostle Paul reminds his readers that when they came to believe in Jesus, God sent the Holy Spirit into their lives. As soon as that happened, they began to cry out to God using the name that we are all encouraged to hold sacred—"Papa, Father." Note how everyone is invited into this relationship. When Paul says "Papa, Father," he uses an Aramaic word (*Abba*, translated "Papa") and a Greek word (*pater* translated "Father"). The Jews spoke Aramaic and the Gentiles spoke Greek. By using words from both languages, Paul reminded us that people of every race are invited to know God as Papa. It doesn't matter what your background is: when you believe in Jesus and receive the Spirit, you get to call God your Dad! No longer are you slaves to the law, trying to measure up. Rather, you are adopted sons and daughters. When that happens, you join a worldwide family of people from every tribe and nation, all of whom know God as "Papa! Father!" just like Jesus did.

PRAYER

*God, I thank You that Your heart is to be a Papa to
people from every nation. I accept the invitation to
know You as my Dad. In Jesus' name. Amen.*

Sons Not Slaves

Doesn't that privilege of intimate conversation with
God make it plain that you are not a slave, but a child?
—GALATIANS 4:7

When a boy was adopted in Paul's day, he was usually bought out of slavery and given the great gift of being his adopting father's actual son and heir. This was an amazing privilege. No longer was the child bound—he was free. No longer was he poor—he was rich. No longer was he hopeless—he was hopeful. No longer was he in danger—he was safe. Being adopted in the Roman Empire of Paul's time was a great blessing! And it is a great blessing today. When you and I were separated from the Father's love because of sin, we were bound, impoverished, hopeless, and in peril. But now, thanks to the adoption price that Jesus paid, we are no longer any of these things. Instead, we enjoy a new Father, a new freedom, a new fortune, a new future, and a new favor. Never forget that adoption is the greatest and highest blessing that the Father bestows. We have gone from slavery to sonship. Now we can enjoy the privilege of intimate conversation with God, addressing Him as "Papa"!

PRAYER

*Thank You, Jesus for paying the redemption price
and, through Your blood, setting me free from the
state of slavery and giving me the position of God's
child. Amen.*

A Joyful Heart

Isn't it clear, friends, that you, like
Isaac, are children of promise?
—GALATIANS 4:28

Paul here reminds his readers of the two sons of Abraham—
Ishmael and Isaac. Ishmael was the result of a union between
Abraham and a slave girl. Consequently, he represents slavery.
Isaac, on the other hand, was the offspring of Abraham and his
wife Sarah, and represents sonship. In his letter to the Galatians,
Paul offers his readers a choice. They can either live in the legacy
of Ishmael, which is slavery, or they can live in the legacy of Isaac,
which is sonship. Those who live in the pattern of Ishmael are
without hope, because they do not enjoy the Father's promises.
Consequently they are hopeless and miserable. Those who live in
the pattern of Isaac have a hope and a future. Consequently, they
are joyful and full of adventurous expectation. Let's never forget:
the Father's plan was to send Jesus to rescue us from slavery and
to give us sonship. So then, live as an Isaac, whose name means
laughter. Rejoice and be happy! You are a son, a daughter, not
a slave.

PRAYER

*Thank You, Father that You want me to be filled with
the joy of knowing that I am an adopted child, with the
promise of a hopeful future. Amen.*

Grace and Peace

I greet you with the grace and peace poured into our
lives by God our Father and our Master, Jesus Christ.
—EPHESIANS 1:2

It's hard to beat the welcome Paul gives to the congregation in
Ephesus. He greets them with the blessing of grace and peace
poured out by the Father and the Son. What is grace? It is, firstly,
the undeserved love of the Father for sinful human beings. When
we were far away from Him, separated from His presence because
of our sin, God sent His Son to die for us so that we could be
brought home into His arms of love. That is amazing grace. But
there's more: grace is, secondly, the presence of the Father's love
in our hearts, empowering us to be like Jesus and do the things
that Jesus did. When Paul uses "grace" in his greetings, he is
unleashing the love of Heaven. In addition, he releases "peace"—
that harmony with the Father, with others, with ourselves and
with our environment, which come to us through Jesus alone.
Next time you greet someone, speak grace and peace over their
lives. These are mighty gifts given by the Father through His Son.

PRAYER

*Father, I cannot thank You enough for Your amazing
grace and Your exceptional peace. Help me to live in
these blessings and to give them away. Amen.*

Father and Son

What a blessing he is! He's the Father
of our Master, Jesus Christ.
—EPHESIANS 1:3

Paul begins his letter to the Ephesians by thanking the Father, describing Him as "the Father of our Master, Jesus Christ." There are two common mistakes Christians make. The first is to love Jesus but neglect the Father. Some people who have been wounded by their earthly fathers understandably find it hard to relate to their Father in Heaven. They therefore talk to Jesus, because He is safe, but ignore the Father, because they're afraid that He will turn out to be like their own fathers. The second error is to relate to the Father but to neglect His Son, Jesus Christ. There are people, believe it or not, who just want to relate to the Father and who forget that, as Paul says here, He is *the God and Father of our Lord Jesus Christ*. This is dangerous: those who split the divine family in Heaven often end up splitting the Lord's family (the Church) on earth. One thing is for sure: we should never divide the Father and the Son or the Son and the Father. They may be separate persons but they are the same being. So never forget: God is "the Father of our Master, Jesus Christ"!

PRAYER

Dear Father, Son and Holy Spirit, help me always to see You as Three-in-One and One-in-Three. Help me to be an agent of unity, not division. Amen.

Whole and Holy

Long before He laid down earth's foundations, he
had us in mind, had settled on us as the focus of
his love, to be made whole and holy by his love.
—EPHESIANS 1:4

Paul is focusing here on the blessings of the Father's love. He tells his readers that way before the Father created the heavens and the earth, He chose us to be the focus of His great love. You and I were chosen for adoption into the Father's love before the world was made. You and I were selected out of the orphanage of this world to become the Father's sons and daughters by adoption. Why did the Father do this? Paul gives the answer. He wanted, from the beginning, a people made whole and holy by His love. Notice the words "whole and holy." Our Heavenly Father wants us to be holy—to live according to the high standards of His Word, not the low standards of this world. And He wants us to be whole—to have all the broken and fragmented parts of our souls restored and reintegrated by His miracle-working love. What a wonderful privilege it is to be the Father's adopted child, growing more and more whole and holy in His love! Isn't that worth celebrating?

PRAYER

*Dearest Father, thank You for choosing me; please help
me to grow more and more like Your Son—whole and
holy in Your love. In Jesus' name. Amen.*

The Father's Plan

Long, long ago he decided to adopt us
into his family through Jesus Christ.
—EPHESIANS 1:5

When a couple decide to adopt a child, they go through a process of planning. They approach an adoption agency that then leads them to a particular child. This can sometimes take time. In the case of our adoption as the Father's sons and daughters, it took a long time! Our Father had a plan in place before the world was made and that plan was to adopt us as His sons and daughters. However, it wasn't until Jesus was born that this plan began to be fully realized. When Jesus died on the Cross, He shed His blood to pay the price for our redemption from slavery and our adoption as God's daughters and sons. After that, He rose from the dead, ascended to Heaven, and poured out the Spirit of adoption when we said "yes" to the invitation to follow Jesus. There may be many unplanned pregnancies in the world, but there are no unplanned adoptions. Aren't you grateful that you have a Father who planned for you to be in His family?

PRAYER

Dearest Father, I cannot thank You enough that You had a plan long ago to adopt me as Your very own child. I praise You for Your awesome love. Amen.

Over the Moon!

What pleasure He took in planning this!
—EPHESIANS 1:5

Long ago, before the foundations of the earth were laid, our Father planned to adopt us as His children, choosing us to become the focus of His love. Paul says here that it gave the Father great pleasure planning this. Have you ever considered the Father's pleasure? Far too many believers have a very low view of themselves, imagining the Father choosing and adopting them with great reluctance—with gritted teeth and clenched fists. When they think of the Father's face, they see a frown not a smile. But Paul takes time to remind us that God is not like that at all. He's a really good Father who has always been indescribably happy about adopting us. This is often something we find in earthly parents who decide to adopt. They will often tell an adopted child, "Some children come out of their mother's tummy, but you came out of our hearts." That is pleasure! Never forget: your Father is over the moon that you're His adopted child.

PRAYER

Dearest Father, please help me, by Your Holy Spirit, to understand more deeply Your great delight in choosing and adopting me. In Jesus' name. Amen.

The End Game

He wanted us to enter into the celebration of his
lavish gift-giving by the hand of his beloved Son.
—EPHESIANS 1:6

As Paul winds up his thanksgiving for the Father's blessings in his opening prayer in Ephesians 1, he turns to the glorious riches of God's amazing grace. In celebrating the Father's lavish gift-giving, He focuses on one monumental benefit of the Cross of Christ—we are now accepted in the Father's beloved Son, Jesus Christ. Here Paul explains the consequences of our adoption, that because we are adopted, we are accepted. Here, in one fell swoop, a death blow is dealt to every attempt to earn the Father's acceptance through works, through striving, through performance. This is what orphans do; they engage in endless efforts to win people's approval. Sons and daughters are not like this. Sons and daughters—including *adopted* sons and daughters—rest in the astonishing blessing that the Father loves them because of their position, not their performance. Let's enter the celebration of the Father's lavish love, that there is nothing we can do to win the Father's love. We already have it. The end-game is to know this and to party in the goodness of it, now and for eternity.

PRAYER

*Father, thank You so much that all I have to celebrate
Your unconditional acceptance is to receive Your lavish
love in Jesus. In His name. Amen.*

Being in Christ

It's in Christ that we find out who we
are and what we are living for.
—EPHESIANS 1:11

Let's ponder for a few moments on the phrase "in Christ." Paul uses this expression frequently. What does it mean? To answer that, let's consider where Christ is now. He is seated at the right hand of the Father, where He lives forever to look into His Father's face, to worship, and pray for all those who follow Him on earth. When you and I are born again, we are gathered by the Holy Spirit into the Son's relationship of love before the Father. Yes, Jesus is the only Son by nature, but we are also sons and daughters by adoption. In Christ we get to do what Jesus does—look into the Father's face, worship Him, and pray according to His heart. Consequently, it is "in Christ" that we find the clue to our identity and destiny. Our identity is tied up with who we are in Christ—sons and daughters of God. Our destiny is tied up with what we do in Christ—bringing the blessing of the Father's loving rule to the nations. Let's resolve to live our lives "in Christ". This is where we get to know who we truly are and what we are on this earth to accomplish!

PRAYER

*Dearest Father, help me to live my life in Christ, so that
I may know I am Your child and that I am called to
share Your love with the nations. Amen.*

No Favorites

Through him we both share the same Spirit
and share equal access to the Father.
—EPHESIANS 2:18

When Paul says "through Him" he means "through Jesus." When he uses the word "both," he means both Jews and Gentiles. Paul was a Jew and he knew that Jews hated Gentiles. The Gentiles were referred to as pagans and regarded as the great unclean. There was even a wall in the Temple that separated Gentiles (on the outside) from Jews (on the inside). What Paul says in this verse is revolutionary. Thanks to the Cross, both Jews and Gentiles can now share the same Holy Spirit, and because of that they both have equal access to *Abba Father*. How radical is that! The exclusion zones have been abolished; the wall has come down. Now everyone, from every tribe and nation, can believe in the Son, receive the Spirit and come into the Father's arms. All women and all men, all children too, can know Papa, Father.

PRAYER

Papa, Father, I thank You that You have no favorites and that You welcome everyone into the holy place of Your presence. In Jesus' name. Amen.

True Prayer

My response is to get down on my
knees before the Father.
—EPHESIANS 3:14

What do you do when you are overwhelmed by the greatness of God and the wonders of His ways? When the Apostle Paul was in this frame of mind, he responded by bowing before the Father. Let's never forget what prayer truly is. It is a heartfelt conversation with Abba Father. Any attempt to make prayer more formal or sophisticated just ends up in religious ritualism and frigid formalism. Prayer was never meant to be like that. Prayer is my adoring response to the Father's overtures of amazing love. It is my "Thank You, Papa." It is my, "I love You, Papa." It is my, "I have things to ask You, Papa." It is my, "I'm listening to You Papa." True prayer is being led by the Holy Spirit into a place where we are so at one with Jesus that we pour out our praise and prayers before the Father, just as Jesus does. True prayer is a loving conversation in the Spirit, through the Son, with Abba Father. Let's make it our priority to get down on our knees before our mighty and majestic Abba Father!

PRAYER

*Dearest Father, please forgive me for trivializing and
formalizing prayer. Help me to engage in heartfelt
conversation with You. In Jesus' name. Amen.*

Planted in Love

I ask him that with both feet planted firmly on
love, you'll be able to take in with all followers of
Jesus the extravagant dimensions of Christ's love.
—EPHESIANS 3:17–18

Paul is busy praying for the people in the church in Ephesus. He
gets on his knees before the Father and asks that they would have
their feet planted firmly on the foundation of love. In the original language, there are two words here: "rooted" and "grounded."
The first is an agricultural word. Paul prays that we would be
like flowers, planted deep in the soil of Abba Father's love. The
second is an architectural word. Paul prays that we would be
like houses built on the firm foundation of Abba Father's love.
Let's establish our lives on the sure and solid foundation of the
Father's love, revealed to us in Christ Jesus and ministered to
our hearts through the loving Spirit of adoption. Then, when
we know this reality ourselves, we can pray for others to come to
know the extravagant dimensions of Christ's love—the ultimate
demonstration and revelation of the Father's matchless love for
the world.

PRAYER

Dearest Father, help me to be rooted like a plant and
grounded like a building in Your great love, revealed to
us in Christ Jesus. In His name. Amen.

Filled With Fire

Drink the Spirit of God, huge draughts of him.
Sing hymns instead of drinking songs! Sing
songs from your heart to Christ. Sing praises
over everything, any excuse for a song to God the
Father in the name of our Master, Jesus Christ.
—EPHESIANS 5:18–20

When it comes to worshipping God, there are some who love structure and there are others who love spontaneity. In truth, the Apostle Paul enjoyed both. As a faithful Jew, he would have said many well-known, formal prayers. As a Spirit-filled follower of Jesus, he would also have uttered many informal prayers. In this verse Paul talks about the importance of being continuously filled with the Holy Spirit. He reminds us that we must go on receiving God's Spirit. This is vital. What pours out of us is evidence of what has been poured into us! Those who are constantly taking huge draughts of the Holy Spirit sing hymns and songs from their hearts to Abba Father, in the name of the Lord Jesus Christ. Hymns are structured. Songs are spontaneous. Whichever kind of music flows out of us, whatever kinds of prayer we utter, it is vital that our hearts are on fire with the Father's love.

PRAYER

Dearest Father, help me to be so continuously filled with
the fire of Your love that my praises and my prayers
pour forth constantly from my lips. Amen.

Positive Reflections

Fathers, don't exasperate your children
by coming down hard on them.
—EPHESIANS 6:4

Fathers have a vital role in the family, a big reason being because they can help or hinder a child from appreciating the Father-hood of God. It is now commonly known that children who are brought up by fathers who are constantly angry find it hard later on in life to believe that Father God isn't the same. Children who are brought up by fathers who engage in excessive discipline and cruel punishments find it hard later in life to believe that Father God isn't like that too. Earthly fathers are like windows onto the Father's heart. It is for this reason, among others, that Paul cautions fathers not to exasperate their children by coming down hard on them. At a purely human level, this will create resentment in the child's heart. At a spiritual level, it will adversely affect that child's ability to relate to God as a good, good Father when that child comes to know Jesus. If you're a father, resolve to be a positive reflection of our Father in Heaven. If you've been poorly fathered, understand that your Father in Heaven is perfect and you can trust Him.

PRAYER

Dearest Father, I worship You that You are the perfect Dad and that I can trust You, whatever my earthly father was like. In Jesus' name. Amen.

A Gratitude Attitude

We can't quit thanking God our Father.
—COLOSSIANS 1:3

If you're a father, you'll know that one of the greatest joys in life is to do something that you know will make your children happy. Maybe it's giving them a certain gift or taking them to a particular restaurant. When that child thanks you without being prompted, when their gratitude simply pours out of their hearts, it is one of the most beautiful things in the world. As a dad, it makes your heart expand with even greater generosity. This is a picture of the Father's heart. Let's remember there is a direct link between gratitude and grace. Both come from the same Latin word, *gratia*. This is a clue! The more grateful you are for the Father's blessings, the more His grace is released in your life. Let's cultivate Paul's mindset of constantly thanking God our Father. He's the greatest Dad in the universe. He has lavished love on us in Jesus. He has continued to be generous in giving the gift and the gifts of His Spirit. Let's thank Him spontaneously and regularly, from our hearts!

PRAYER

Dearest Father, help me to be a person known in Heaven for my gratitude attitude. Help me every day to enter Your gates with thanksgiving. Amen.

You Raise Me Up!

It is strength that endures the unendurable and
spills over into joy, thanking the Father who
makes us strong enough to take part in everything
bright and beautiful that he has for us.
—COLOSSIANS 1:11–12

The Christian life can often be extremely arduous. The enemy
of our souls is constantly at work trying to distract and depress
us, to dismay and destroy us. One of the hallmarks of being an
adopted son or daughter of God is therefore suffering, but in
this, as Paul points out here, our Father doesn't leave us to go it
alone. Far from it! He empowers us by His Holy Spirit with a
mighty strength to bear the unbearable. This strength then spills
over into an outrageous joy. Instead of being weighed down and
crushed by our circumstances, the Spirit gives us the strength to
rise above them. With this perspective, we then getting thanking Abba Father that He has given us the privilege and the
power to partner with Him in the brilliant assignments He has
for us. In our own strength, we could never do this. But in Abba
Father's strength, we can sing, "I am strong when I am on Your
shoulders!"

PRAYER

*Dearest Father, in Your strength You raise me up so I
can stand on mountaintops and walk on stormy seas. I
cannot thank You enough. Amen.*

No More Separation

I'm absolutely convinced that nothing—nothing
living or dead, angelic or demonic, today or
tomorrow, high or low, thinkable or unthinkable—
absolutely nothing can get between us and God's love.
—ROMANS 8:38–39

Romans chapter 8 is one of the greatest chapters in the entire
Bible. It begins with Paul saying that there is no condemnation
for those who are in Christ Jesus. Once we have decided to follow
Jesus, we receive total forgiveness as we believe that the penalty
for our sins has been paid in full at Calvary. If this wasn't good
enough, the same chapter ends with the fantastic truth that there
is now no separation for those who are in Christ Jesus. Nothing in either the supernatural or the natural realms of life can
separate us from the Father's love. What amazing grace this is!
And what reassurance this is for anyone who has experienced
the awful agony of separation from an earthly father. Thanks to
Jesus, we are never going to be separated from the Father again.
Absolutely nothing can come between us and Him. Paul says he
is "convinced" about this. Let's not just believe this. Let's be convinced about it too!

PRAYER

Dearest Father, I am so encouraged by this glorious
promise. Nothing will ever separate me from Your
fatherly love. In Jesus' name. Amen.

Happy Saints

*We'll be a choir—not our voices only, but our very
lives singing in harmony in a stunning anthem
to the God and Father of our Master Jesus!*
—ROMANS 15:6

The greatest English preacher of the nineteenth century was
Charles Spurgeon. He once distinguished between unhappy and
happy saints. He said that unhappy saints believe that God is a
Master and we are His slaves. They operate with a religious kind
of Christianity which is highly legalistic. He rightly saw that such
people are profoundly unattractive to people outside the Church
because they are miserable. Happy saints, however, are completely
different. They revel in the fact that God is their loving Heavenly
Father and that they are His beloved children. Consequently,
they are joyful because they are free, not bound by religious ser-
vitude. Such people, Spurgeon said, are contagious when it comes
to those outside the Church. Such people, to use Paul's words
here, are like a wonderful choir. They are like the most outra-
geously gleeful Gospel singers, getting unbelievers up from their
seats to dance and sing, joining in with a stunning and harmoni-
ous anthem to Abba Father. Don't you want to be a happy saint?

PRAYER

*Dearest Father, deliver me from the misery of religion
and release me into the contagious joy of relationship
with You. Through Jesus I pray. Amen.*

Living for Abba Father

There is only one God the Father...everything
comes from him, and...he wants us to live for him.
—1 CORINTHIANS 8:6

In Paul's day there were many pagan religions on offer, including the myth-based religions of the Romans and Greeks. In religions such as these, gods like Zeus were sometimes referred to as "father," as in the phrase "father of the gods." Paul, however, is adamant. These are demonic counterfeits of the God and Father of our Lord Jesus Christ. There is only one who deserves to be addressed as *Abba* Father. Everything that exists comes from Him because He is the Creator of everything. This Father has a longing in His heart that we should come to recognize Him as our Father and that we should spend all our lives living for the One who gave us life. Living for *Abba* Father is only possible through Jesus. Jesus Christ revealed the true Father and reconciled us to this Father at the Cross. All other gods that are described in fatherly language are deceptive distractions. Our Father in Heaven is the world's greatest Dad and the Father we've all been waiting for—the Father who loves us like no earthly father ever can. Let's live for Him.

PRAYER

*Dearest Father, I want to satisfy the deepest longing of
Your heart and live for You alone. I will not follow any
other gods. In Jesus' name. Amen.*

Nobodies and Somebodies

Take a good look, friends, at who you were when
you got called into this life. I don't see many
of "the brightest and the best" among you.
—1 CORINTHIANS 1:26

Remember how the Father chose Israel out of all the nations of the earth because of His love, not because of their size or their achievements. In this we learn something very important about the Father's heart. He does not choose significant people—He chooses insignificant people. He does not choose extraordinary people—He chooses ordinary people. This has always been the Father's way of operating. As with Israel, He selects ordinary people and does extraordinary things through them. That is why Jesus chose 12 ordinary men and changed the course of history through them. This is a demonstration of the Father's heart—to take hold of nobodies and turn them into somebodies. That is why the Apostle Paul could say to the church in Corinth, "You weren't the brightest and the best in society when God called you!"

PRAYER

*Thank You, Dearest Father that You choose ordinary
people for an extraordinary privilege and an
extraordinary purpose. In Jesus' name. Amen.*

Father of Compassion

Father of all mercy! God of all healing counsel! He comes alongside us when we go through hard times.
—2 CORINTHIANS 1:3–4

What is compassion? Compassion is a combination of two Latin words—one means "together with" (*com*) and the other means "suffering" (*passion*). When someone displays compassion, they come alongside someone in need or in pain to bear the burden with them. This is what God is like. He is the Father of compassion. He is not aloof and apathetic, because in Jesus Christ He has come to live with us, to suffer and die with us. In Jesus, God has become Immanuel—not God above us, or God against us, but God among us, walking where we walk, feeling what we feel. What a wonderful thing it is to know that when we suffer hard times, our Father is right there with us. He comes alongside us because He is the one who has come among us in Jesus, suffering with us too. As we listen to this Father in our hurts and hardships, He whispers His healing counsel to us, enabling us to find the comfort and resolve to endure. Let's open our hearts to the Father's compassionate love in every season of difficulty.

PRAYER

Dearest Father, thank You that You are an empathetic Father and that You don't stand aloof from my pain, but feel deeply what I feel. In Jesus' name. Amen.

The Gift Giver

Every desirable and beneficial gift comes
out of heaven. The gifts are rivers of light
cascading down from the Father of Light.
—JAMES 1:17

Sometimes we pursue things that are not beneficial to us. It is the devil who puts these idols in our path. His plan is to entice us with them, then to entrap us and finally to enslave us. James teaches that such things are worthless. They lead only to destruction and death. However, what our Father offers us brings growth and life. These gifts are far more healthy and attractive than anything the devil has to offer. The devil's enticements come from hell. The Father's gifts cascade down from Heaven, where the Father of Light reigns in the brilliant glory of His majesty, supremacy and generosity. Yes, I said "generosity." Our Father is extravagantly generous! Let's never be seduced by the counterfeit gifts that the devil places in our path. Rather, let's continually gaze up into the adoring eyes of our Father in Heaven and receive from His bountiful heart the gifts that are the source of our truest, noblest, and purest desires. Let's worship the Father of Light, not fall for the father of lies!

PRAYER

*Dearest Father, I give You the highest praise because
You are the most extravagantly generous Dad and all
that I need is in You. Amen.*

I See You

God the Father has his eye on each of you.
—1 PETER 1:2

A good father keeps an eye on his children. He doesn't do so in an intrusive or an abusive way, looking out for our mistakes so that he can punish us, waiting for moments of failure so that he can beat us up. No, a good father looks out for his children, making sure that they do not go down a dangerous and destructive path, making sure that they have everything they need to fulfill their purpose. God is like this too. He is the most perfect Father and, as such, He has His gaze turned toward our lives all of the time. In the Old Testament, one of the Father's names is Jehovah Roi, the God who always sees us; the God who continually watches over us, night and day (see Gen. 16:13). Aren't you grateful you have a Father in Heaven looking out for you with eyes of love? Aren't you comforted by the fact that your Father looks down from Heaven and says, "I see you, son; I see you daughter"? Our Father is constantly watching out for us, helping us to fulfill our calling and obey His will.

PRAYER

Dearest Father, I thank You that I don't just gaze at You. You also look at me, keeping an eye out for my well-being all of the time. In Jesus' name. Amen.

What a Dad!

What a God we have! And how fortunate we are
to have him, this Father of our Master Jesus!
—1 PETER 1:3

Sometimes you've just got to praise Him. This is what the Apostle Peter is doing here. He has been expressing his gratitude that God is a loving Father who watches over His children. Now Peter turns this into adoration. "What a God we have!" What a statement that is. When you think of the God whom we worship, you just have to say, "Wow!" "Wow" could be short for "Worthy Of Worship!" And He is. Jesus has shown us. Jesus came to reveal that God is our *Abba* Father. He is the Father who loves us perfectly, unconditionally, relentlessly. He is the Father we've all been waiting for all the days of our lives. Peter gives Him praise—this Father whom Jesus reveals; this Father to whom Jesus reconciles us. Sometimes you've just got to praise Him. As you grow in your appreciation of how fortunate you are to have Him, why not exclaim, "What a Dad I've got!"

PRAYER

*Dearest Father, I am truly so blessed to have You as
my Father. What an incomparable Dad You are, the
Father of our Lord Jesus Christ. Amen.*

The Threefold Blessing

The amazing grace of the Master, Jesus Christ,
the extravagant love of God, the intimate
friendship of the Holy Spirit, be with all of you.
—2 CORINTHIANS 13:14

Don't you just love the way Paul finishes this letter? Paul releases three blessings. First, he speaks the blessing of the amazing grace of Jesus Christ. Jesus is the Son, so this is the Son's blessing: amazing grace, the self-sacrificial love of Jesus Christ that empowers us to do what we are called to do. Then, second, he speaks the blessing of the extravagant love of God. "God" here refers, as often in Paul's writings, to the Father. So this extravagant love is the Father's blessing. Then, third, Paul speaks the blessing of the Holy Spirit. Intimate friendship is the Holy Spirit's blessing. If we want to bless another, then we can do no better than give the gift of this threefold benediction. These three blessings are the blessings of the Triune God—the God who is Three-in-One and One-in-Three. These three blessings are blessings of relationship, releasing the love of Jesus, the affection of the Father, and the friendship of the Spirit into our lives. Let's get blessing one another!

PRAYER

Dear Father, Son and Holy Spirit, help me to enjoy the blessings of Your love, affection, and friendship, and give these blessings away to others too. Amen.

Intimate Communion

> We saw it, we heard it, and now we're telling you so
> you can experience it along with us, this experience of
> communion with the Father and his Son, Jesus Christ.
> —1 JOHN 1:3

What is the Apostle John saying here in his first letter? Keep in mind that he was an eyewitness of all that Jesus said and did. He saw with his own eyes a rabbi from Nazareth relating to God as His Father. More than that, he saw with his own eyes the way God related to Jesus as His one and only Son. John was so overwhelmed by this that he wrote the Gospel of John to celebrate this "experience of communion." Notice the word "experience." The relationship that Jesus had with His Father was experiential. Too often in our Christian lives we settle for a relationship with God that is cognitive, not affective; it touches our minds but not our hearts. Not so Jesus. He experienced the Father's love. Furthermore, this experience was one of constant communion—an unending flow of intimate love between the Father and the Son. As John says, this is something we can experience too, just as he has experienced it!

PRAYER

*Dearest Father, help me not to settle for second best and
relate to You only in my head. Help me to commune
with You in my heart. Amen.*

Enjoying The Father

Our motive for writing is simply this:
We want you to enjoy this, too.
—1 John 1:4

In the previous devotion we saw John talking about the "experience of communion" between the Father and the Son, and between the Son and the Father. He was an eyewitness of this. He wrote about it in his Gospel. In his first letter, John now tells us that he and others enjoy this experience of communion with the Father. More than that, the reason why he is writing is because he longs for his readers to experience it too. This of course means us! We too can enjoy communion with the Father. We too can experience a relationship with Abba Father that is felt in the heart, not just known in the head. Yes there may be a difference between Jesus and us. Jesus is, after all, the Son by nature, while we are sons and daughters by adoption. But adopted kids get to enjoy their dad's love just as much as the biological kids do! Let's therefore make it our aim, as Abba's adopted children, to life a life of communion with our Father. Let's not settle for anything less.

PRAYER

Dearest Father, I want to enjoy the same experience of communion with You that John experienced. Help me to know more of Your love. Amen.

The Propitiator

*If anyone does sin, we have a Priest-Friend in the
presence of the Father: Jesus Christ, righteous Jesus.*
—1 JOHN 2:1

The scientists who invented the space shuttle created tiles to cover much of the belly of the craft. These were made out of the sand of the desert—the only substance on earth able to tolerate the heat of reentry into earth's atmosphere, and the freezing cold on the dark side of the moon. Every time the astronauts reentered our atmosphere, these tiles took the heat. Now that is quite some invention! At NASA, its nickname is "The Propitiator." In the case of our lives, Jesus Christ died on the Cross in our place, absorbing in His body the fire of the Father's righteous anger over human sin. Jesus, in short, was—and indeed *is*—our Propitiator. That is why the Apostle John says that if we do sin, we have a Propitiator ("Priest-Friend") who stands in the Father's presence—the Righteous Jesus. Let's resolve not to grieve our Father's heart by sinning, but if we do, let's remember that Jesus took the heat for us. Consequently we can reenter the atmosphere of the Kingdom of Heaven—the Father's presence.

PRAYER

*Dear Lord Jesus, I thank You from the depths of my
heart that You are my Propitiator and that You took
the heat for me. In Your name. Amen.*

Personal Experience

You know the Father from personal experience.
—1 JOHN 2:14

Let me tell you about my father. He was an extraordinary man. He was very brave in World War II. He was a prisoner of war for three years. Then he came back to England and studied at Oxford University. He dined with C.S. Lewis every week for two years! He committed his life to Christ during that time. He then wrote a book about his war experiences called *Return via Rangoon* and became a teacher of English Literature. He and his wife Joy adopted my twin sister and me in 1960, and brought us up with great kindness. He died in 1997, and I still miss him to this day. Why am I telling you this? It's because I knew my adoptive father from personal experience. The same is to be true in our relationship with God. We are not just to know about Him—we are to know Him in our hearts. He is the Father who has adopted us. We are His beloved children. People need to say about us what John said about others: "You know the Father from personal experience."

PRAYER

Father, thank You that You long for us to know Your love personally. Help me to know You more clearly and love You more dearly, day by day. Amen.

An All-Consuming Passion

Don't love the world's ways. Don't love
the world's goods. Love of the world
squeezes out love for the Father.
—1 JOHN 2:15

Getting to know our Heavenly Father doesn't just mean draw-ing closer in love to Him. It also means learning to be more like Jesus in every way. This is why John stresses that those who try to love both the Father and the world will never succeed. It's either one or the other. Genuine love for the Father eclipses all other affections in our lives, so much so that every desire in our hearts is subsumed beneath the one overriding priority, which is to love the Father with all our heart, mind, soul and strength. Nothing less will do. This is what Jesus did as the Son by nature, and this is what we must do as the sons and daugh-ters by adoption. In setting our highest affections on the Father, it becomes impossible to have space in our hearts for any other object of worship. All idols must go. Love of the world squeezes out love for the Father, but love for the Father also squeezes out love for the world. Let's every day make it our aim to displace love for the world with the Father's all-sufficient love.

PRAYER

*Dearest Father, forgive me for those times when I love
the world too much. Help me always to love You more
than anything or anyone. Amen.*

Conquering Sin

Practically everything that goes on in the world—
wanting your own way, wanting everything for
yourself, wanting to appear important—has nothing
to do with the Father. It just isolates you from him.
—1 JOHN 2:16

A person cannot love the world and love the Father. When John uses the word "world" (*kosmos* in the Greek), he uses it in a negative way to denote the earthly realm where human beings exist and where sin reigns, not just in our hearts but in our social systems. When a person loves the world, sin takes hold of their hearts. This leads to us worshipping idols like sex, money and power. The trouble with this is that it separates us from the Father's love. As John says here, "It just isolates you from him." This is the greatest possible tragedy. In an earlier devotion we saw how nothing can separate us from the Father's love. When Paul says "nothing," he means "no external force." He did not mean sin. When we sin it separates us from the Father's love. Sin is an "internal force." Sooner or later we all have to make a choice. What will we pursue in life—love for the world or love for the Father?

PRAYER

*Dearest Father, help me to understand the power of
sin to isolate and separate me from Your love. Give me
grace to live a holy life. In Jesus' name. Amen.*

Affirming the Son

No one who denies the Son has any part
with the Father, but affirming the Son
is an embrace of the Father as well.
—1 JOHN 2:23

No one can experience the Father's love unless they first accept
and confess that Jesus of Nazareth is the Messiah and the Lord of
lords and King of kings. If a person denies that Jesus is the Christ,
there is absolutely no way they can ever know God as Father, let
alone experience His amazing grace and His loving embrace.
Anyone who claims to have any kind of revelation of the Father
outside of an eternal friendship with Jesus Christ is deceiv-
ing themselves. If you think about it, this is blazingly obvious
and perfectly logical. Only the Son can reveal the Father. Only
this same Son can reconcile you to the Father. There is no other
source of revelation. There is no other agent of reconciliation.
Everyone who pursues the Father's heart, therefore, passionately
defends and declares the fact that Jesus is the Messiah and that
Jesus is Lord. Anyone who denies the Son, or who fails to affirm
the Son, will never embrace the Father. Let's be sure to continue
to give Jesus the highest honor.

PRAYER

*Dearest Father, I know that there are many who do not
recognize who Jesus really is. Help me to continually
affirm that Jesus is Lord. Amen.*

Deep Calls Unto Deep

*If what you heard from the beginning lives deeply
in you, you will live deeply in both Son and Father.*
—1 JOHN 2:24

Jesus once compared the person who shares the Gospel, with a farmer who sows seeds in the soil. The seeds that go deep take root and grow. Those that only drop into the surface get eaten by the birds. The lesson is this: we must let the words of Jesus go as deep as possible into our hearts and minds. Let them be so embedded in our souls that we remember them every day and apply them obediently in our lives. If we do, we will live deeply in both the Son and the Father. So, the deeper we let the teaching of Jesus take root in our thinking, the greater our friendship will be with the Lord Jesus and the Father. This is the reward for continuing and growing obedience to the true truth of the Bible. We get to know Jesus better, and we get to know our Father better too. Let's make sure that our hearts are deeply submitted to the Word of God so that, in turn, we may enjoy the deepest communion with the Son and the Father.

PRAYER

*Dearest Father, I want to live as deeply as I possibly
can in You and in Your Son. Help me to let Your Word
dwell deeply in my heart, I pray. Amen.*

Doing Right

All who practice righteousness
are God's true children.
—1 JOHN 2:29

There are those who stress the Father's love, and there are those who stress God's righteousness. Rarely do you find the same person emphasizing both. However, Jesus did. In John 17 He prayed to God as "Righteous Father." For Him there was no polarization of holiness and love. He knew that God was both loving Father and righteous King. This has radical implications for us as God's adopted children. We have to understand that a true child of God not only enjoys the Father's embrace, but also pursues the Father's righteousness. As Jesus said, seek first the Kingdom of God *and His righteousness*. Many like the idea of pursuing God's Kingdom, but not so many like the idea of pursuing God's righteousness. If we want to be authentic children of the Father, then we must "practice righteousness." We must say and do what Jesus would say and do in every situation. This commitment to a love-based holiness will mark us out as the true children of our Heavenly Father. So let's commit to pursuing purity as well as intimacy.

PRAYER

*Righteous Father, help me to prove that I'm Your child
by not only enjoying Your embrace, but also by always
doing the right thing. Amen.*

An Integrated Faith

God's firm foundation is as firm as ever, these sentences
engraved on the stones: God knows who belongs to
him. Spurn evil, all you who name God as God.
—2 Timothy 2:19

Here the Apostle Paul likens God's truth to the foundations of
a house. On the foundation stones there are two inscriptions.
Notice the theme of these two stones. The first is intimacy: "God
knows who belongs to Him." The word "know," as so often in
the Bible, carries a relational nuance. Another way of translat-
ing this inscription would be, "Dad knows His kids!" The second
inscription is all about purity: "Anyone who claims to know God
as Father should always avoid sin." The adopted children of God
make sure that both of these truths are written on the foundation
of their hearts. They daily cultivate their intimate communion
with the Father who knows them in love. They daily steer clear
of sinful choices, and make sure that they never rebel against the
Father's love. Let's have both of these truths engraved upon our
hearts. Let's integrate intimacy and purity in our lives.

PRAYER

*Dearest Father, give me grace to nurture both intimacy
and purity, I pray. Help me to know Your love and also
to follow Your ways. Amen.*

The Love Center

There is no room in love for fear. Well-
formed love banishes fear.
—1 JOHN 4:18

In pursuing holiness, we must be very careful not to live from a center of fear. There are far too many religious people in the world whose reason for trying to obey God is because they have a terror of being punished. But fear is a very poor motivator. It is far better to live from a center of love. Fear says, "I'm terrified of God, therefore I'm going to strive to stay the right side of Him." Love says, "I know that my Father in Heaven adores me, therefore I'm going to please Him by doing the right thing." These two mindsets are poles apart. The first is utterly toxic, and leads to a feeling of never measuring up, never being good enough. The second is profoundly healthy and leads to blessed assurance. We need to make sure that we live righteous and holy lives, not to avoid punishment, but rather to avoid breaking the Father's heart. When this happens we want to do what pleases Him because we live to make Him happy.

PRAYER

Dearest Father, help me always to find out what pleases You, and pursue that out of love. Please drive out all fear from my heart. In Jesus' name. Amen.

Resting in Abba's Love

We, though, are going to love—love and be loved.
First we were loved, now we love. He loved us first.
—1 JOHN 4:19

There are two centers from which we can live our lives: fear and love. Those who live from fear are always afraid of other people's disapproval, including God's. This leads to them striving constantly to earn acceptance—an exhausting and depressing way to live. Then there is the center of love. Those who live from love are secure in the fact that the Father approves of them. They rest in the fact that the Father loves them, likes them, and is especially fond of them. They know this because Jesus has demonstrated and proved it on the Cross. As John puts it here, "He loved us first." This is so important. We cannot give love to others if we are not secure in the knowledge that we are truly beloved. This is John's point. We do not live out of a fear of God's disapproval and punishment. We live out of a revelation of His unconditional love and affection. It is because of this that we love others, including our sisters and brothers in the family of the Church. So let's love and be loved!

PRAYER

Dearest Father, I thank You so much that You first loved me. Help me to rest in the certainty of that love, so that I can freely love others. Amen.

Honoring God's Family

If anyone boasts, "I love God," and goes
right on hating his brother or sister,
thinking nothing of it, he is a liar.
—1 JOHN 4:20

One of the hallmarks of a child of God is the fact that they are committed to belonging to a church family and to loving their brothers and sisters in Christ. A true child of God values interdependence. They love to be part of a church family, because they recognize the importance of obeying the command to love one another. A person who is still a spiritual orphan is the opposite. They promote independence, not only in their words, but also in their actions. They do not want to belong to a group of people where they might have to be accountable in love, let alone show their love for others in actions that speak louder than words. This is a very dangerous attitude. John says that anyone who hates their brother and sister in Christ, who stirs up division in the family of God, who wants to go it alone and live on their own terms, is deceived. They are liars. Let's make sure we put the highest possible value on loving our adopted sisters and brothers in Christ. Let's love, not hate, the Father's family.

PRAYER

*Dearest Father, forgive me for any independent and
proud attitude in my heart. Help me to honor Your
family and love my brothers and sisters. Amen.*

A Part, Not Apart

"Obedience is thicker than blood. The person who
obeys God's will is my brother and sister and mother."
—MARK 3:35

When you think of the Church, how do you picture it? One of the most beautiful pictures of all is the family. If you think about it, this makes perfectly good sense. If Jesus reveals that God is our loving Father, then what does that make us? It makes us the adopted sons and daughters of God. If that is true, then we are in turn brothers and sisters to each other. Jesus said as much in this passage. He declared that the community that He was forming was not one defined by blood relationships, but by obedience to God. Anyone who chooses to follow Jesus becomes part of His family on earth. They become his "brother and sister and mother." When you and I choose to follow Jesus, we do not do this independently. We join a family of people who have chosen to obey the will of our Father in Heaven. Those who are spiritual orphans hate this. The true children of God, however, delight in it.

PRAYER

*Dear Lord Jesus, I want to be a member of Your family
on earth. I ask that You would help me to be part of a
church, not apart from the church. Amen.*

Loving Authority

Don't be harsh or impatient with an older man.
Talk to him as you would your own father, and
to the younger men as your brothers. Reverently
honor an older woman as you would your
mother, and the younger women as sisters.
—1 TIMOTHY 5:1–2

Why do we need to belong to a local church? We live in an age when everyone wants to do what is right in their own eyes. Consequently, more and more believers are living like orphans—doing whatever they want, avoiding any kind of oversight, however loving, and promoting independence. Not only is this destructive, it is totally disobedient to the Word of God. In the passage above, the Apostle Paul is speaking to Timothy. Timothy is a younger man who has chosen to be accountable to Paul, his spiritual father. Paul tells Timothy to exercise authority in love, treating others with the same honor as he would give to members of his own family. This is how every church is meant to be—led by people who are filled with the Father's love and filled with people who joyfully submit to loving authority. Let's resolve to be under loving oversight in the church. Let's also be determined to exercise oversight with love.

PRAYER

*Dearest Father, please heal me of any wounds inflicted
by churches, and help me to receive and give the kind of
oversight that truly reflects Your love. Amen.*

Encouraging Each Other

> Let's see how inventive we can be in encouraging
> love and helping out, not avoiding worshiping
> together as some do but spurring each other on,
> especially as we see the big Day approaching.
> —Hebrews 10:24–25

If a person claims to know the Father heart of God and yet refuses to be a part of a local church family, be wary of them. The author of the letter to the Hebrews warns us that there are those who avoid worshipping God with other Christians and who just go it alone. This is a clear sign that they are still thinking as spiritual orphans. The writer reveals what kind of thinking is embraced by the person who is truly God's child. Such a person is creative in encouraging and helping others out in the Church. They love worshipping together with their brothers and sisters in Christ. They really love spurring each other on to even greater obedience to the Father as the big Day approaches. What Day is that? It is the Day when Jesus Christ will return. On that Day He will honor those who have honored Him, and His family on the earth.

PRAYER

Dearest Father, help me to place a very high value on
meeting with my brothers and sisters in Christ and
spurring each other on to higher heights. Amen.

Abba's Discipline

It's the child he loves that he disciplines;
the child he embraces, he also corrects.
—HEBREWS 12:6

Being Abba's child not only means we get to receive His embrace, but it also means we get to experience His discipline. This is one aspect of the Father's heart that tends to be neglected. Most people only want to hear about the Father's delight; they don't want to learn about the Father's discipline. However, this is all part of the process of growing up. This process usually involves three stages: first of all the Father reveals in Jesus that He loves and embraces us. Then, once we know His affection, our Father takes us through times of refining. These are seasons of character development, designed to help us lay down everything that hinders us from being the best son or daughter that we could be. When this is over, a third phase begins, where we begin to see the fruit of all this discipline in a greater holiness of life and a greater productivity in our destiny. Growing into maturity as a son or a daughter of Abba Father not only involves experiencing His affection; it also involves experiencing His correction. Let's remember that it's the child the Father loves that He disciplines.

PRAYER

*Dearest Father, I thank You that You reveal Your love
before You minister Your discipline—that way I can
truly trust You in the process. Amen.*

Worth It All

"Conquerors will march in the victory parade, their names indelible in the Book of Life. I'll lead them up and present them by name to my Father and his Angels."
—REVELATION 3:5

Jesus promises that one day, those who conquer will march in the victory parade in Heaven's Kingdom. When Jesus comes back to earth on the last day of history, He will take us into the very presence of the Father and present us by name—not only to our Father, but also to His angels. "Father," Jesus will say, "let me introduce Mark to you. He was a faithful warrior for the Kingdom of Heaven on earth. He fought for you till the end of his life." "Father, let me introduce Helen to you. She was a godly mother who raised her children to know and love the truth." "Father, let me introduce Rick to you. He wrote stories all his life that brought glory to Your name and released Your light into people's hearts." What will the angels do when this is going on? I believe they will be applauding, cheering and dancing with joy. In the end, it will all be worth it. Never surrender! Never quit! You're a conqueror!

PRAYER

Dearest Father, when I feel like giving up, help me to fix my eyes upon the prize, when Jesus will present me before You in Heaven. Amen.

Coming Home

> "Conquerors will sit alongside me at the
> head table, just as I, having conquered, took
> the place of honor at the side of my Father.
> That's my gift to the conquerors!"
> —REVELATION 3:21

When we go away for a long time from our families, from those whom we love, it is a truly wonderful thing to return home. The very word "home" is powerful. It warms the heart. The Bible is full of homecomings, but none more beautiful than the home-coming of the Son of God. When Jesus Christ died for our sins, the Father raised Him from the dead by His Holy Spirit, and lifted Him to the highest place in Heaven where He sat in the place of honor next to the Father. What a homecoming that was! But there's more. God's adopted sons and daughters will come home too. We are going to enter the Father's house and be escorted into the largest dining hall in the universe. There we will sit with Jesus Christ at the head table. As Jesus says here, "That's my gift to the conquerors." We may face some defeats in our lives, but let's make sure we finish well. We don't want to miss out on a homecoming like this!

PRAYER

*Dearest Father, I'm excited about the banquet that
awaits Your conquering daughters and sons. May I be
numbered among them too. Amen.*

Coming Down Again

I heard a voice thunder from the Throne: "Look!
Look! God has moved into the neighborhood,
making his home with men and women!"
—REVELATION 21:3

The Bible reveals that when Jesus Christ returns, everyone will be raised from the dead with new resurrection bodies. After that, everyone will be judged at the throne of God. Some will live in perpetual separation from the Father's love, while others will live in His presence forever. After that, the old earth and heavens will be purged and transformed into new heavens and a new earth. When that is complete, we will not go up to Heaven; Heaven will come down to earth. God will move into our neighborhood. God will come down to where we are and make His home with us. This is so important. If you are a son or a daughter of the Father, you are not going up to Heaven when you die. Heaven—which is where the Father dwells and reigns—is coming down to where you are! This is the Father's heart: He always seeks to come down to where we are, rather than expecting us to go up to where He is!

PRAYER

*Dearest Father, I cannot wait for the day when Your
Son returns and You come to live with us in the new
heavens and the new earth. Amen.*

Our Glorious Future

> "He'll wipe every tear from their eyes. Death is
> gone for good—tears gone, crying gone, pain
> gone—all the first order of things gone."
> —REVELATION 21:4

When the Bible teaches us about our adoption in Christ, it tells us not only about something past and present, but something future too. Yes, we were adopted as sons and daughters at the Cross—that is the past. Yes, we are continually growing as adopted sons and daughters—that is the present. But one day we will also receive the same inheritance that Jesus received—we will be given resurrection bodies that will never need a doctor, a dentist, or an undertaker—that's the future! When Jesus Christ comes back to earth, we will enjoy the fullness of our adoption. We will no longer commune with the Father indirectly, as we do now in our mortal bodies. We will see the Father face to face, and He will wipe every tear from our eyes. There will be no more sighing, no more crying, and no more dying. We will be alive for evermore in the ultimate intimacy—face-to-face friendship with the Father, the Son, and the Holy Spirit. What a great and glorious future this is!

PRAYER

*Dearest Father, I thank You that, for us, death is not a
hopeless end, but an endless hope. Thank You for this
glorious future. Amen.*

The World at Our Feet

"I'll be God to them, they'll be
sons and daughters to me."
—REVELATION 21:7

Remember what we learned earlier about the practice of adoption in the time of the New Testament. The Jews did not have a rite of adoption, but the Romans did. This involved an adopting father standing before a Roman magistrate and buying a boy from his biological father, usually out of slavery. Once that boy was purchased, the magistrate declared that the boy was *sui heredes*. That is a Latin phrase meaning, "his (the adopting father's) heir!" No longer was the boy an impoverished slave, with no hope for a future. He was now the son of a freeman, with a glorious inheritance. The world was at his feet. This is a picture for us too. Once we were slaves to sin, doomed to die. Now we are the adopted sons and daughters of our Father in Heaven, destined to live forever with Him. That's why our Father promises, "I'll be God to them" and "they'll be sons and daughters to me." All we have to do is to finish our lives well. Overcomers will be overwhelmed by love.

PRAYER

Dearest Father, I am so excited about the thought of coming into my inheritance. Help me to be victorious in all my battles. Amen.

An Epic Calling

The anxious longing of the creation waits
eagerly for the revealing of the sons of God.
—ROMANS 8:19 (NASB)

Never forget, Jesus came not only to save us *from* something, He came to save us *to* something. When we put our trust in Him, we are redeemed *from* sin and adopted *into* sonship (this includes daughters too). What we need to realize is that the whole of creation is waiting for those who have entered into the fullness of what it means to be the adopted sons and daughters of Abba Father, because we carry the glorious freedom of the children of God. This freedom is not for us alone. It is for the entire creation, which is waiting with eager anticipation for our appearance. Creation pines for this because it knows that our manifestation is tied up with its own liberation. This is an epic calling, and it is precisely why the Father's heart can never be a fringe topic—it is absolutely foundational. The whole cosmos is waiting for us to grasp it! May we continue to walk in the reality of our identity as Abba's daughters and sons, so that we may truly set the captives free until the day that Jesus returns!

PRAYER

*Dearest Father, I thank You for the supreme honor of
being called Your son, Your daughter. Help me to bring
freedom wherever I set my feet. Amen.*

Dr Mark Stibbe is an award-winning Christian author who has over 30 popular books and five academic books in print. His first book was a collection of poems (published when he was 16). Many of his popular books have been best sellers and his academic books are required

reading in universities and seminaries all over the world. Recently Mark has taken to writing works of fiction and is currently collaborating with his friend G.P. Taylor to develop a series of novels about an English Vicar who reluctantly becomes a secret agent in the time of the French Revolution and the Napoleonic Wars.

Mark has given himself to coaching writers and has been running a service called The Script Doctor. He is now the CEO and founder of KWS (Kingdom Writing Solutions), a holistic service for writers. He is also a popular contributor at writers' conferences and workshops.